DRESS YOURSELF

Viviane Williams

WeBook Publishing - English Edition

Published by WeBook Publishing – Los Angeles, CA

This work is based on the author's experience while trying to adapt to a new country and fashion culture. At the same time, unfolding the secrets of Image Consulting. Embark on a journey of authenticity and feminine confidence guided by Viviane's personal and professional story. Understand how psychoanalysis can illuminate your self-awareness, guiding fashion choices that reflect your essence. The author intends to help you express yourself through fashion and image. The methods described within this book are the author's personal findings. You may discover there are other methods and materials to accomplish the same end result.

For information, please email info@webookpublishing.com

First English Edition

ISBN: 979-8-9886684-4-2
LCCN: 2024912645
Written by Viviane Williams
Translator: Laura Linn
Copy Editor: Ana Silvani
Cover Art: We Do Marketing
Cover Designer: Gabriel Prada
Interior Formatting: WeBook Publishing

Manufactured in the United States of America

Contents

Acknowledgments

To her who often sacrificed her time and energy so that we had everything we needed, whose qualities - loving, helpful, loyal, kind, among many others - make her such an incredible woman, whom I can call Mom - Naibel, thank you. Without her, this new chapter wouldn't be possible. Besides giving me life, she also gave me an older sister, Elaine, who behaves and acts like a mother to me as well and whom I love dearly. She supports my ideas, even from afar, and nearly gave me a heart attack by surprising me with a visit to Los Angeles in May 2020. She accompanied me on trips to Paris and has been there on all the most important occasions in my life. And to my father, José Artur, who always expresses his love with countless questions about how everything is going here and wants to know every detail of my American life.

I thank my husband, Tyler, for all the love, affection, support, and strength he always gives me to achieve my life goals and to better our marriage. He has been a gift from Jehovah God in my life and has been amazing in this adaptation process here in California. Today, besides being a great family, we are the best team. Also, I thank my father-in-law, Reggie, for all the support he and my brother-in-law, Marlon, have given me during this new phase over the past five years. And Jackie, who also provided the support I needed during this time. Undoubtedly, these have been the most challenging years and the ones that have taught me the most about being brave, moving forward even when afraid, and knowing that I am never alone.

Jennifer, Mike, Isabelle, and Lillah, who welcomed me, became family, and who also are part of my growth here in the United States. Thank you so much!

And finally, I thank all my friends. I won't mention names so as not to forget anyone, but all of them, without exception, are part of this incredible journey. Thank you for everything; without your support, this journey would have been even more challenging.

Today's date: _____

How would you describe your image?

_____
_____
_____
_____
_____
_____

How important is your image to you?

_____
_____
_____
_____
_____
_____

What results did you seek from reading this book?

_____
_____
_____
_____
_____
_____

Introduction

"What you have, everyone can have, but what you are, no one can be."

Costanza Pascolato

Where would you start telling your story? Looking back can be difficult, and depending on how your life has been, you might not want to take that pause. But, thinking it over, it's how you built your values, attributes, and qualities. It's in this way that you forge a strong personal image. My story strengthened my image, and I will tell you how.

However, this book is not just an account of my restarting, changing, and rediscovering journey. It's a revelation of how I embraced this new experience with a renewed perspective, turning challenges into opportunities and bringing an inspiring image consultancy business to life. Through these pages, I share my personal evolution, how I developed my image consultancy method and all the growth and creativity along the way. I am passionate about image consultancy and love to write about my deepest feelings. It's as if each page is an honest conversation with myself, where I share joys, sorrows, and challenges and open my heart sincerely and truthfully.

My move to California marked the beginning of a path that transformed not only my geographical location but also my personal life. Alongside Tyler, my husband, I embarked on a journey that revealed my courage. Even though I felt so much fear at times, I also had a lot of determination, especially in my spiritual goals. Tyle's constant support reminds me every moment that I am never alone; he holds my hand firmly and is always by my side, a partner, a friend, a husband, and a love that I always wished for.

This new phase also awakened a deep nostalgia for my family in Brazil, especially for my parents, Naibel and José Artur, and my sister Elaine. The longing became a constant companion, and the first months away from them proved challenging. Despite this, our daily video calls made it possible to be present, even from a distance, reinforcing the value of love and the bonds we've built.

During this period, I discovered an inner strength I didn't know I had, a determination intensified by the distance, which drove me to achieve more than I ever imagined. I developed my image and style consultancy method that goes beyond the external, allowing each woman to know her personality better. When we know ourselves and can see our essence, it lets us look at ourselves more confidently. But this method would not be possible if I didn't have my friend, partner, and the best psychoanalyst I found to help my clients bring out the best in each one.

I met Blenda through Instagram on December 27th, 2022, and I saw what she did as intriguing and precisely the differentiator I was looking for in my business. After our first video call, she immediately agreed to be part of my team. Today, we strengthen this unique method with our singularities. I, Viviane, am the image consultant, helping women enhance their appearance and style. Blenda, as a psychoanalyst, assists women in understanding their deep personalities and building an image that truly reflects who they are. Together, we combine visual transformation with emotional self-knowledge, providing our clients with a holistic and powerful approach.

I also developed a networking group where I bring the Hollywood reference to this event, allowing all women to understand that they, too, deserve an Oscar. Therefore, I need to honor all the women present at the first event held in Recife on January 16, 2024, a truly special and memorable day. So, my deepest thanks to my mother, my sister, Blenda Ribeiro, Magali Rattacaso, Janessa Pascoal, Agatha Martins, Emile Luna, Denise Maria, Gessica Rattacaso, Roberta Monteiro, Karoline Monteiro, Mayara Albuquerque, Carol Araujo, Teresinha Araujo, Daniela Oliveira, Mila Moura, Carol Malucelli, Cristiane Feitosa, Shirley Araujo, Natalia Costa, Fabia Melo, Lany Santos, Milena Carla, Micheline Rocha, Tamiris Tavares, Flavia Regina, Karla Bruno, the restaurant Studio Mu and Chef Mateus Uchôa who made that night unforgettable with dishes paired with wines.

Reading this book will make you look at your personal image differently. Beyond worrying about the best look, you will start to care about the fundamental piece of personal image: yourself! I hope you understand how important it is to develop your self-knowledge to learn to dress more confidently and build a strong image, not only concerning colors, trends, or fashion, but seeing yourself in a more sensitive, respectful, and careful way—from the inside out—after all, you are an emerald!

Viviane Williams

What do I want to share with you right now? You will be moved, you will learn a lot, and you will make your image more valuable. By the end of this book, you will become a stronger woman who desires to value your story, your values, and especially your name.

The judgment of a good or bad personal image often depends on the context and circumstances in which it is presented. It's crucial to remember that these are merely generalizations, and each person is unique, with a singular combination of characteristics that define their image.

Chapter 1
A Brief Retrospective

"Give a girl the right shoes, and she can conquer
the world."

Marilyn Monroe

How many times have you w shed to change your life? How many times have you looked in the mirror and realized you deserved more or could give more of yourself but felt you weren't capable? When you stop and look around, how often have you wanted to start over in another country? Begin training? Change the way you dress? Develop good habits? Have a new routine? We always want something new, yet we often remain stuck and blame time, lack of money, or other circumstances for our lack of results.

Often, we don't know where to start. We are bombarded daily by information, courses, and feeds that update every second, yet we remain in the same place. There are many open doors, and you don't know where to go, what to follow, what to do, or whom to emulate. Are you the person who seized all the opportunities life brought and now enjoys a good life, the fruit of your process and patience? You were afraid but dared to face it!

But, to those who didn't open the door out of fear of failure or what others might say—what has changed in your life? I've always been fearless, known as "You're crazy. I wouldn't have that courage."

No change is easy, and it always brings butterflies in the stomach, like being on a roller coaster, right? We get excited until we get close, but when it comes to those final moments of 3, 2, 1... We want to quit out of fear. It might not seem like it, but we do the same thing in life. Can I share something? I've felt that way, too, but the difference is that I took the plunge. What about you? Want to dive into this story and see how brave and daring I was?

If you ask, "But Viviane, weren't you scared?" I'll answer in the same second: "With every thought and breath, my heart was in my mouth, and my world was falling apart." Maybe it's better to say I was VERY AFRAID. But the decision is yours—to be paralyzed by fear or to take your foot off the brake and let yourself live?

Often, the obvious needs to be said: courage is not the absence of fear. Courage is being afraid and moving forward anyway. When faced with fear, the best thing to do is calm down, breathe, and keep confronting each stage of life. So, grab your favorite drink—tea, water, coffee, wine, juice, mate—sit somewhere that brings you peace, and come live this story with me. The difference is you'll leave here feeling beautiful, confident, and more encouraged.

Ready? Then, come with me!

A Fresh Start and an Effective Method

To understand why I needed courage, let me tell you about the difference in how our qualities and vulnerabilities reflect on our image. I also learned how my life and image changed when I started focusing more on myself, understanding myself, and realizing that despite being brave, fear held me back for many years. One of those fears was the fear of being myself. Today, I'm much more interesting when I'm myself than when I try to be someone different, adapt to people around me, or force a personality that makes others happy. At the same time, I wasn't true to myself, perhaps to fit into certain social circles or relationships.

I've realized that recognizing my strengths has shown me how amazing I am, and this isn't arrogance or lack of humility—in fact, it took a lot of therapy to accept and see myself this way. Now, I'm not afraid to voice my opinion, but of course, I consider the feelings of others and how I present myself without trying to appear superior because I'm not. It's important to talk about this, or better, to write about it.

One day, I met the love of my life.

Hold on, this isn't a romantic comedy book. I didn't imagine that July 5, 2019, would change my life, but it did. First, because I had been in other relationships before and in therapy, I understood that I lacked self-confidence, which reflected negatively on everything in my life, especially my image. Well, I started talking to a man who seemed very Brazilian, but I was tricked because he was actually American. But it was okay, and it was meant to be just a chat and nothing more. After all, I wasn't looking for anyone at that moment unless it was God's choice because I believe that when we trust and put God first in our lives, He always helps us make good decisions. Today, I see that it was indeed a gift from Him for my now-husband and me because one year later, on the same July 5, we got married.

Meeting Tyler was more challenging due to our very different time zones. I couldn't understand everything when we talked, so we mostly texted during the day because it was easier to translate and understand each other. One habit we had that helped us get to know each other better was studying biblical topics together to prepare for the challenges of marriage. This allowed us to see each other's opinions on various subjects and understand where we agreed or disagreed. We did this once a week, and every night, he would call me before bed and say a prayer for us to make good decisions in our relationship. I began to understand English more, even though speaking it was still challenging.

After a few months of talking, the first choice and act of courage was: "Where are we going to live? Brazil or the United States?" At that moment, my world stopped as if it were a movie, and I tried to foresee my future to get an answer, but I couldn't. "How can I live far from my family and friends? Here in Recife, I know everything. I have my job, my life." But after a few seconds, the answer was "California" because he already lived there, and it would be better for both of us. I didn't even know what I was saying, I just wanted the chance to start over, as if I could start my life from scratch, and that's literally what happened.

It should be noted that my husband offered to move to Brazil, but when we weighed everything, like Tyler's profession, which he wouldn't be able to practice in Brazil, and the safety and quality of life, we concluded that living in the

United States would be better for both of us. I must confess that I wasn't prepared to move to another country, leave my culture and language behind, and this was a quick but very difficult decision. I barely spoke English, and I spoke less than the basics, and we mostly communicated through Google Translate. When he visited Recife on October 26, 2018, we went out to dinner since it was close to the date he would return to California. It was hilarious because usually, our friend Janessa acted as our translator, but she wasn't there that night; so, when it came time to order dinner, I couldn't understand what Tyler wanted to eat, and to make matters worse, our internet wasn't working! After a few minutes, we got internet access and, With the waiter's help, we finally placed our order. At the end of the night, Tyler gave me a promise ring, and yes, once again, he tried to speak a few words in Portuguese. We had such a fun evening. Oh! And the worst—or maybe the best—part is that a couple of friends, who are now our godparents, Giovane and Magali, were at the same restaurant just in case we needed help with translation. But instead of helping us, they let us deal with the struggle while watching from afar and laughing at the situation.

July 16, 2019: the day had come for me to leave and say goodbye to my entire family, and I didn't know what to feel. It seemed like the world I was given at birth was collapsing while simultaneously being rebuilt by me. Many friends and relatives cried with me at the airport after a beautiful wedding and several farewells. When I boarded the plane, it felt like half of my heart had been ripped out and shattered on the tarmac. The pain was intense, even though the choice was mine.

Do you know what I wore to board the plane that day? A sweatsuit. Why? It gave me the comfort I needed to calm my heart at that moment. I didn't know when I might return, and I had no certainty about what lay ahead. Would I dress that way today with all the image knowledge I have now? Possibly not. Looking back, I can't believe that's what I wore.

Depending on the context, a sweatsuit can reflect neglect, relaxation, comfort and has a more casual approach. At least it was monochromatic and chic, reflecting those overcast days when all you want is a hug and your family's lap. But that's exactly what I was leaving behind at the airport gates in Recife.

When I landed in California, once again, my world fell apart. I couldn't believe the courage I had to leave my family. Tearful phone calls accompanied each layover. And so began my new life. During the first few days, it felt like I couldn't believe that change had happened, and I didn't feel that space belonged to me. The first feelings of insecurity began to surface. You don't need to move to a different country to experience such emotions; you might have felt them in other situations. I initially felt like I had lost myself; I no longer recognized who I was. Life had brought me there and taken away my independence. I needed to restart, and even though I didn't know where to begin, I had to keep going. I know many people can adapt quickly, as I'd see on Instagram, where everyone appeared so happy and successful so soon here, but the truth is, well... not everything shown is real. If you've spent years building your life in your country, how can you rebuild it from zero in just four years? Keep in mind, in the first seven months, I couldn't even drive!

On August 12, 2019, I started studying English and needed my husband or father-in-law to drive me around. Although life had to go on, the anxiety from waiting for travel documentation approval heightened my distress. I often thought, "When will I be able to see my family again?" My mother's visa was denied twice, and my world crumbled! That natural pain reflected how unsettled my psyche was, even though my marriage was happy. Then the pandemic hit, adding more anxiety—borders closed, no one could enter or leave the country. "Now what? When will I see my family?" This question was on repeat, and my husband kept asking me to trust in Jehovah God and that everything would be okay.

Each step of the immigration process moved slowly, making me cry, as it felt like a countdown without knowing the exact day I'd return. Then, I received permission from the U.S. government to travel out of the country during the pandemic. Despite the surrounding uncertainties, I decided to visit my family. On March 26, 2021, I boarded my first flight after a year and a half away—but it felt like five years! I know many people living abroad spend much longer before returning to Brazil. I was so anxious about that trip that I packed almost 20 days in advance! Around eleven in the morning, I received a message from the airline saying I needed to get to the airport earlier because my original flight was delayed and I wouldn't make the connection. My heart almost jumped out of my chest! I called my husband, but he said he couldn't leave earlier than our scheduled time to take me to the airport—it was about an hour from our house, and no one else was available to drive me. So, I had to wait. Having worked in aviation, I started searching for other flight options because I couldn't miss that trip—it was my chance to see my family. That couldn't happen, especially on that day.

But I had no other choice but to wait. Once my husband arrived, I was already waiting at the door, and we headed to the airport. Upon arrival, the airline staff informed me that I wouldn't make my connection and could only travel the next day. At that moment, my world collapsed; I couldn't believe I had to go back home and wait another day after almost two years post-pandemic, which left us very shaken.

Returning home, I was even more devastated, and the worst part was that I couldn't share it with my friends because they didn't know I was traveling to Brazil. The next day, I managed to board the flight. After a long journey (changing clothes at each layover due to the virus), I could finally hug my family again. But nothing was the same because now I had a *Half Love** heart (or life)—if I were in the U.S., I would miss everything in Brazil, and if I were in Brazil, I'd miss my husband, who stayed home in California. (*Bilingual poetry book *Half Love, Metade Amor* by Ana Silvani)

It was evident that reuniting with my family and friends made me very happy, but it was also clear how confused my mind was when it came to dressing. It didn't matter what I wore; what mattered was that I was with my family and enjoying their company. I cherished those two long weeks, which felt like the quickest of my life. Then, it was time to return and suffer the distance again, but I would face my feelings alone this time. That's what I needed to come back even stronger and focus on building my life.

Life went on, and I began to observe how American women dressed and groomed themselves—always with eyelashes, long nails, sweatpants or leggings, and sneakers—they always conveyed a sense of comfort. I wanted to start wearing those clothes, too, perhaps as a way to fit into this new world and adapt. But in a way, nothing made me feel at home in my new universe: that style wasn't mine, even though the choice was mine. I still felt lost, trying to find direction through everything around me, what was trendy or what I simply thought looked good on me.

My mind was a mess. The brave woman I believed I was would lock herself in the room after English classes and just cry. There was nothing to do, and the worst part began: my desire to dress up diminished. I only wanted to stay in pajamas, and I no longer felt the urge to put on makeup. But I was happy—thrilled in my marriage—so why was this happening? In truth, despite the joy of finding an incredible husband, I was lost within myself. I didn't recognize the woman staring back at me in the American mirror. I didn't understand or know where to begin rebuilding my life.

For example, whenever my husband invited me to dinner, I never knew what to wear. I never felt I had the right clothes for the occasion, never felt beautiful. I tried on countless outfits, and even when he told me I looked beautiful, I didn't feel beautiful or confident in what I was wearing. Seeing him always well-dressed and elegant made me feel even less secure.

In Brazil, the Viviane I was used to seeing in the mirror was always well-dressed—or so I thought. Later, I realized that my posture and the way I spoke always conveyed insecurity. When there were no other outfit options for going out, I would borrow clothes from my sister. But now I see that even when I appeared well-dressed, it still didn't represent me. I wasn't dressing as my true self. That wasn't the woman reflecting who I was—always proud and presentable, with my nails, hair, and eyebrows always done. So, what was the problem? Everything was quite visible, but I couldn't see it; the problem was that I wasn't emotionally well, so I didn't like anything I wore. I kept trying on clothes, but nothing felt right.

Are you thinking that it's because I didn't have options? No, I was genuinely insecure, and it was obvious, but I couldn't see it.

Looking in the mirror revealed truths I tried to hide all the time. But it was in the shower that my image of strength crumbled under the weight of longing, uncertainties, and insecurities. Each challenge that arose made my heart race; I didn't feel capable. I couldn't trust myself to do anything or have good ideas because the anguish of uncertainty and the new (which never stopped being new) lingered for a long time and made me cry.

It was a race against time, with a pounding and anxious heart and restless thoughts surrounding me, even though I wanted my image to reflect something different. The reality was that I couldn't keep lamenting my longing, my insecurities, or any negative thoughts that tried to demotivate me. I don't like being sad; to me, it's ike wasting a day of living, even though I know it's important to go through these moments. It's often in pain that we find the solution or the key to happiness.

I started identifying my priorities and began doing volunteer work. Helping others has always made me very happy. I feel much happier when I see the smile of someone I've helped than when I receive a gift. After setting my priorities and improving my English, I searched for what I genuinely love to do.

Viviane Williams

Since I already had a degree in Business Administration from Brazil, I considered studying Accounting here in the United States because it seemed like a natural complement and might make it easier to find a job. However, it would have restricted my ability to visit my family, and even while taking the Accounting course, I realized it wasn't what I wanted to do. In a conversation with my therapist, I asked, "What kind of work can I do here?" Her only advice was, "Try to find a job where you can help people." That made me think a lot: "Wow, it would be really cool to find something that allows me to help people. That would be amazing!"

I thought about opening a Brazilian-style store to help women dress in a way that reflects and improves their emotional well-being. However, I felt discouraged when I looked at all the costs involved. Additionally, I wanted all the pieces to be my own creations. I started studying the subject intensely, planning, and researching, but nothing got off the ground, and the months continued to pass.

One day, my friend called and asked for help organizing her suitcase because she was going to spend twenty days in Europe with just a carry-on and didn't know what to pack. Some countries would be colder, and others warmer. I hadn't considered that could be a job until I started taking a course about branding. My mentor asked us to position ourselves within the market. I needed to pause and say, "Well, my store isn't happening yet, but if I help women dress well, starting with their emotional well-being, that's something new to this market."

I began researching extensively how our emotions influence what we wear when we open the closet. That's when I found an article discussing our emotions' impact on our clothing choices.

According to the site *Coaching Psychology*, applying psychology to fashion is considered an emerging field in psychology. In Brazil, the Federal Council of Psychology does not even recognize it as a specialized area of practice.

Therefore, the field of Fashion Psychology (read more: careerpsychology.org), as it's being called in London and New York, is still in its pioneering stages. So far, there are two major references in the global application of psychology to fashion: Dawn Karen and Carolyn Mair.

The Advancements of Dawn Karen:

Dawn Karen is a Columbia University (New York) psychologist who combined her modeling experience with her psychological knowledge. She spent about a year traveling around the world conducting research and case studies. During this period, she mainly studied the cultural components of dressing, the influences of cultural norms on how we dress, and how this affects our emotions and behaviors.

For Karen, "Fashion Psychology" is about understanding why people wear what they wear and the effects our clothes have on others, as well as on our own thoughts and emotions. The application of psychology in fashion and personal image integrates psychological science and its therapeutic tools with knowledge from these fields.

In summary, personality, self-perception, the people we interact with, and how we relate to them are the main factors impacting our relationship with fashion, purchasing decisions, and how we present ourselves to the world.

Realizing this, I understood I needed to help women with an innovative and exclusive image consulting service. But how could I do that? Initially, I would need someone trustworthy to care for my clients, and they had to be willing to test the method to see if it truly worked and understand how self-awareness impacts them. One day, while browsing Instagram, I found Blenda. She talked a lot about personality traits, which I found interesting. I immediately sent her a message, and shortly after, she responded, and we set up a meeting. She was enthusiastic when I shared my idea with her, and we started working immediately. It felt like a dream coming true. I realized that all the initial pain transformed into a great idea, culminating in a partnership that strengthened our image consulting service.

During my professional image and style consulting course in Paris, I learned the importance of asking questions like: How do I see myself? How would I like to be seen? How do I think others see me? These questions complement my approach to image consulting and reinforce my belief in the importance of understanding our self-perception and the projection of our image.

In the next chapter, I will delve deeper into the concept of image and how these fundamental questions play a crucial role in how we present ourselves to the world.

Chapter 2
Authentic Image

"Beauty begins the moment you decide to be yourself."

Coco Chanel

When you think about image, what's the first thing that comes to mind? Maybe it's an unforgettable moment, like the birth of your baby, your wedding day, the moment you dedicated your life to God or your spirituality, or perhaps a personal achievement. All these moments bring to mind a happy image. However, when we talk about image in the context of consulting, some people still think it only refers to how we dress. Actually, our image goes way beyond the clothes we wear; it expresses feelings, preferences, tastes, personality, and emotions. This means that taking care of our emotional well-being is as important as paying attention to what we wear.

Moreover, it's essential to understand that our image isn't just about external appearance but also an internal manifestation. Reflect on this: do you want to draw attention to yourself or go unnoticed on a sad day? You probably go for the latter. This happens because, when we choose what to wear, our emotional state shows through in some way. When we are balanced inside, it clearly reflects in our appearance. Thus, it's essential that when we aim to improve our image, we consider not only our physical appearance but also our emotional and mental state. After all, when we feel good inside, it also shows outside.

It's also interesting to notice how our perception of our own image influences not just how we see ourselves but also how we feel about ourselves and how we present ourselves to others. We radiate a positive and secure presence when we feel confident and comfortable with our appearance. On the other hand, a negative self-image can affect our self-esteem and social interactions. Therefore, when discussing image, it's crucial to consider both the external and the internal perspectives and how they shape our view of ourselves and our place in the world.

According to the Oxford Language Dictionary, an image is a representation, reproduction, or imitation of the form of a person or object, a particular aspect by which a being or object is perceived, a scene, or a picture. In other words, the image covers not just the physical appearance of someone or something but also the perception and interpretation that appearance provokes. This brings us to three important characteristics of image:

1. Our Physical Appearance:

It is the most obvious image aspect because it refers to our outward form, including characteristics like color, shape, size, and texture. For example, how we dress, style our hair, or present ourselves physically.

2. Perception:

It is how people see and interpret us, and it can vary widely based on culture, social context, and individual experiences. For instance, an elegant outfit in one culture might be seen as inappropriate in another. In many Western contexts, more revealing clothing like short shorts, low-cut tops, or swimwear is common. It may be appropriate in specific settings, such as beaches, parties, or informal gatherings. In contrast, in some Middle Eastern cultures, especially in conservative Muslim countries, these same outfits could be considered inappropriate or even offensive. In these cultures, people are expected to dress more modestly, reflecting cultural and religious values.

3. Interpretation:

Education, personal values, and beliefs influence interpretation. For instance, one person might interpret a facial expression as a sign of happiness, while another might see it as sarcasm.

Think about how many times your mom, spouse, or kid had an expression you interpreted one way, but they told you it wasn't what you thought. It happens quite often.

Making sure your physical appearance is perceived and interpreted correctly is important to avoiding any misunderstandings in your image and conveying the message you want. So, ask yourself: How do I see myself? How do I think others see me? How would I like to be seen? Revisiting these questions can help you understand your main image goal.

When you ask yourself:

How do I see myself? What comes to mind right away? Recognizing that over the years, you can develop a deeper understanding of "Who am I?" Both emotionally and in terms of style and personality, is crucial. While I used to see myself in a limited way, I now understand that my image reflects much more than just my clothes. It's an expression of my feelings, concepts, and the emotions I've experienced and will continue to experience.

How do I think others see me? For a long time, I believed that my image was defined solely by the clothes I wore. Throughout this journey, I realized that people can interpret my image in many ways, often beyond what I could imagine. This made me reflect on the importance of conveying my true essence in everything I do because we are often judged before we even speak.

How would I like to be seen? I want to be recognized not just for my external appearance but for my authenticity, principles, confidence, creativity, and integrity. I want my image to clearly and genuinely convey my essence, inspiring others to feel secure and confident.

It's interesting to note how the process of self-discovery and acceptance plays a key role in building our personal image. When we deeply understand and value our essence, it naturally reflects in our external appearance. The journey of self-awareness often leads us to reassess our priorities and realize that true beauty comes from within, not from designer clothes or expensive accessories.

"What makes a person chic is not what they have,
but how they behave in life."
Gloria Kalil

When we look at our process of change and growth, we can see how each stage of this emotional evolution manifests in our image. This awareness allows us to develop a more holistic approach to image consulting, focusing not just on external appearance but also on our internal strength.

Just like in psychoanalysis, where we gain new perspectives by observing other people's issues more clearly, seeing ourselves objectively can strengthen us, helping us grow in self-knowledge and resilience. And this deep understanding of who we are enables us to convey security and confidence through our image, inspiring others to do the same.

When I started to examine my process of change and adaptation, I realized how much my emotional evolution was naturally reflected in my image. I developed an innovative consultancy by focusing on women's essence, helping them understand their personality, as well as their physical and mental health, to become more secure and confident. They can strengthen themselves by understanding how they function and seeing themselves from an external perspective.

Often, when we talk about image, there's a conflict between what someone wishes to convey and what they actually show. Many times, attitudes and behaviors don't align with a person's inner essence, creating a noticeable discrepancy. My consultancy emphasizes the importance of understanding your true identity—who you are, your tastes and preferences—and helping you align your external appearance with your inner self. Through a careful process of self-discovery and analysis, we work together to eliminate this discrepancy or noise, ensuring that the image you project to the world is an authentic reflection of your values, personality, and goals. This makes your presence more cohesive and impactful, enhancing personal and professional perceptions.

I wish you can look in the mirror confidently, truly knowing who you are, recognizing your uniqueness—the special touch that makes a difference in any setting you enter. With courage and without fear, convey your true self without hesitation. Don't try to imitate someone you see on social media, in magazines, or on TV because often that person isn't what they seem. Your style is unique; after all, each of us has a distinct uniqueness that should be explored and authentically expressed in our image rather than copied from someone else's style.

"Knowing ourselves frees us from the obligation to act, to maintain an image that is not ours, to live a story whose main character we buried in some chapter long ago. Knowing ourselves liberates the person we are and empowers us to simply exist, embracing our competencies and vulnerabilities." (REIS, Joel & MAZULO, Roseli. *Management and Image*, 2017, page 39)

It's vital to show confidence and comfort when choosing an outfit for any occasion, just as with other important life decisions—where to travel, what to study, where to spend holidays, what career to pursue, or which career transition to embark on. Trusting yourself and your choices is crucial. We live in a time when people are becoming more courageous about doing what they genuinely love. With or without fear, they know they can change. Unlike in the past, when changes might have seemed absurd because everyone was expected to follow the career path their families did or imposed as a synonym for success. Where is your "self" in everything you do? Where is your essence? Does your image reflect what you desire? That's why it's so beneficial to understand the entirety of what makes you who you are so that when it comes time to dress, people can see the incredible person you are right from the first moment. The important thing is to dress as yourself.

I believe no single career can fully express who you are, nor is there one "right" outfit for looking great; after all, nothing can be more valuable than what you do for yourself. Self-knowledge deepens as we explore different aspects of who we are. We may think we know ourselves well enough until we face experiences that challenge us to look inward. For example, examining our bone structure can reveal connections between our history, the people in our lives, and our psychological traits. From there, you start to understand your fears and main characteristics. This helps bolster your self-confidence, which feeds your self-esteem and reflects on your self-image. The attributes that make up your image are a crucial sequence, and skipping any of these aspects can leave something wanting, like your non-verbal communication, what you're wearing, your style, behavior, etiquette, attitude, and confidence.

Let me ask you, dear one —are you ready to be yourself without fear?

Let me share a bit more of my story, and you'll understand when I realized I had courage. Sometimes, even when you think you have it, it's tough to leave your comfort zone.

When was the last time something made you step out of your comfort zone?

For me, it was moving to California and having to relearn practically everything. It felt like hitting the restart button, and my life began anew with the chance to do everything better, bringing along all the experience I had gained in Brazil. When I had to go to school to learn English, I was vulnerable because I couldn't express my feelings precisely, and people wouldn't understand me. When I had to get a new driver's license after driving for nine years and had to learn new traffic rules—like it's okay to turn right on a red light here—it was simple, but it paralyzed me due to its unfamiliarity. I could choose to reinvent myself or rely on the knowledge I gained from studying business administration for four years in Brazil. I decided to pursue what gave me more freedom and allowed me to help women more directly.

Stepping completely out of my comfort zone made me realize how brave I am to learn so many new things in such a short time. Often, as the days go by, we need to remember or appreciate these small achievements we accomplish in a new country with a different culture and language. But what comforted me most was seeing how helpful the Americans I met were when they didn't understand what I was saying. They appreciated my effort much more than I did.

Stepping out of our comfort zone brings emotional instability because of the judgments others might pass or our own insecurity about whether things will work out. We can only gain that certainty by stepping out of our current situation. Often, we want to take action only when everything is perfect, but then we make two mistakes: waiting for perfection that doesn't exist and procrastinating, which keeps us stuck. What do you usually do? What do you tend to choose?

This hesitation prevents us from moving forward or even recognizing the journey we've already traveled, and we forget that every step taken was a journey out of our comfort zone.

Our image's success starts when we positively impact ourselves by looking in the mirror and feeling confident. As a result, we manage to convey authority, confidence, professionalism, and credibility, aligning our values with our image. That's why paying attention to external and internal details is essential rather than just picking anything to wear. You can look in the mirror with tired eyes from a busy day and know you managed to convey all your competence aligned with your best version of each day. Your image begins even before you turn off the lights to sleep, in those moments when you take time to care for yourself. Yet, this is often when we neglect our self-care due to daily stress and a lack of patience. It's important to recognize that, even in moments of fatigue and haste, taking time to care for our image can significantly affect our emotional well-being and self-esteem.

Taking care of our image is a daily exercise. I don't know if your mom used to say, "Home habits go to the street," or if you tell your children that. This well-known proverb in Brazil makes complete sense when it comes to our image. Do you know why?

Because the clothes we choose to sleep in say a lot about how we care for our image, it's the starting point of our self-care. We often love that old, torn nightgown because it holds sentimental value or feelings we don't want to let go of. If that's the case for you, why not start caring for your image by choosing a nightgown that makes you feel beautiful when you look in the mirror before bed? It makes a huge difference. Try it.

One night, I looked at myself in the mirror before going to bed, and since it was freezing, I put on a sweatshirt my husband had given me that used to be his. After a few days, I started feeling unattractive and said to him, "Honey, I need different sleepwear for the winter," and he responded, "Oh! But why? It looks fine on you."

Now, observe the impact my change had on him. I went to Brazil and decided to buy new sleepwear. I chose something that made me feel comfortable, warm, and, of course, beautiful. When I returned to California and put on the new pajamas, my husband said, "Wow, honey, you look stunning!" At that moment, I smiled, remembering his previous comment about the old nightgown looking pretty. By swapping it with something more elegant, I caught his attention. It confirmed what I had mentioned earlier: the importance of caring for our image, even when we're alone, with someone, or just preparing for bed. After all, this is our time to rest and recharge for the next day.

The care we put into our routine, from a simple skincare regimen to the conscious selection of the food we consume, directly reflects on our health and well-being. Similarly, regular physical exercise strengthens our body and nourishes our mind. Thus, every small act of self-care significantly impacts our quality of life.

How much have you looked at and cared for yourself lately?

We often think we need a lot to have a good image, but in reality, beauty lies in simplicity. You make a positive first impression through the whole package you present. It's your life story expressed in your attire, conveyed in three seconds to create an instant impact. But remember: to make any impression, you must like yourself first.

I moved to another country, crossing geographical borders and language barriers. Here, I frequently hear different languages spoken by people from diverse backgrounds. The same is true of universal fashion styles. No matter where we come from or where we're going, we all share our self-expression and authenticity through our style.

Embrace Your Style

For a band to play harmoniously, each musician must know the musical notes and correctly interpret the chords. Similarly, to express ourselves through fashion, it's crucial to understand the "chords" of our style. These "chords" are like verses of a poem that guide us and help us convey the message we want to send to the world. They encompass physical characteristics, the silhouette of each individual, and the key pieces that make up our unique style. Moreover, just as accessories complement an image, they are like the cherry on top, adding a unique and distinctive touch to our appearance.

Discussing style is like uncovering someone's essence, and I invite you to embark on the journey of discovering your own style. However, you need to take an Image & Style test, considering a predominant style and two complementary ones.

A glamorous woman is proud, authentic, powerful, independent, and has a strong, imposing feminine style. Her characteristic is not being classic because she wants to show off her body a bit more without being vulgar. The key piece is to shape the body and highlight feminine curves in a subtly apparent way, with necklines and always remembering the red lipstick. Fitted clothes that show more shoulders, legs, and arms compose her style. Her shoes bring femininity but always with a touch of boldness. The makeup is noticeable, with more striking eyes and red lipstick. This sensual yet non-vulgar style tends to have more visual weight. **This woman's style is sexy.**

She is a glamorous woman who exudes power, modernity, sophistication, and an air of magnetism, as she never goes unnoticed. She brings sophisticated creativity with a classic influence. Her pieces will always communicate this refined modernity with elaborate fabrics and something distinct, whether it be prints, geometries, or a unique designer. Uniqueness is present in her asymmetric-cut shirts, impeccable shoes, and pieces with greater visual weight. Her makeup features well-done skin and dramatic lipstick choices because she is a striking, modern, or urban woman. **This woman's style is modern/urban.**

She is a self-assured, bold woman with a lot of personality who loves the freedom to create and be fashionable. She doesn't want to follow the norm as she unconventionally mixes patterns. She loves exaggerating and contrasting colors without any problem. Using her creativity, this woman knows how to mix prints, create combinations, and use uncommon fabrics. She never walks by without making you turn your head to see her vibrant, joyful colors, carrying big or small accessories, geometric shapes, or sometimes more classic pieces in her looks. She brings visual originality to her choice of shoes. Yes, she is different and unique. **This woman's style is creative.**

This woman is sweet, gentle, detail-oriented, helpful, light, calm, and proud. She composes her look with bows, frills, and florals. She prefers pieces that accentuate her femininity, such as dresses, skirts, lace, and flowy fabrics. She values subtle fits in her body. Therefore, she ensures her makeup is beautiful yet enhances her natural features. Her accessories need to convey delicacy and subtlety, but her vanity doesn't allow her to leave the house without earrings, necklaces, rings, or bows. Yes, her sweet demeanor perfectly matches her light and breezy style. **This woman's style is romantic.**

A woman with a confident, secure, and cultured demeanor who knows what suits her, pays attention to details, values good quality products, appreciates simplicity, and likes to look impeccable.

For this woman, being well-dressed is essential to feeling good. Hence, she chooses tailoring that fits perfectly with impeccable finishes. She likes silk and classic tailoring.

Makeup is a must, and her accessories need to be jewelry or semi-precious. Her hair needs to be well-styled to make her feel beautiful. This clean and polished look brings elegance to her style. **This woman's style is refined.**

A woman who likes to be reserved and conservative, exuding a solid and respectful image. She prefers discretion and timelessness, favoring minimal details and pieces that reveal little skin and withstand the test of time. After all, these choices reflect the consistency of her values and preferences throughout her life. She loves pieces with discreet finishes. She adores fine tailoring, midi dresses, straight-leg pants, and shirts. **This woman's style is traditional.**

A fundamental element in the image of both women and men must be built and is considered a luxury item in the market: CREDIBILITY. It's the primary key element clients often seek, and if you don't have it, you want to acquire it. Conveying credibility through your image is crucial because it instills trust and respect. But how can one achieve this?

By establishing and strengthening your credibility, you are investing in a powerful asset—the trust that others place in you and the value you bring to your personal and professional relationships, which can open doors and create many opportunities. However, building credibility is not a quick or easy process. It requires consistency, transparency, and a continuous commitment to excellence in all your interactions and achievements. Additionally, it's essential to remember that credibility is not just about earning others' trust but also about maintaining it over time. It means acting with integrity, keeping promises, and taking responsibility for any mistakes.

One benefit of solid credibility is the ability to influence and inspire others. For example, a credible leader can motivate their team to achieve desired goals and overcome challenges in a work environment. In social settings, a respected and trustworthy person can inspire friends and family strongly, encouraging them to pursue and achieve their goals. People seek your opinion and follow your advice when you are recognized as an authority in your field. Moreover, credibility can open doors for collaborations, partnerships, and business opportunities that might not otherwise be available. Companies and individuals value reputation and credibility when deciding whom to do business with.

Chapter 3
Embrace Who You Are

"Confidence is the best outfit; you must wear it every day."

Diane Von Furstenberg

Dress Yourself

It was challenging to find self-love amidst insecurities and uncertainty about my path. Questions echoed in my mind: "Who am I, after all? What professionally makes me happy at this moment?" While my spiritual priorities were clear, the professional aspect remained shrouded in mystery, confusing me. Each question felt like an endless labyrinth, a challenge for which I needed clear answers. So, I began to study English and researched how to open a business here in the United States. The idea of opening a clothing store that catered to all styles but in an exclusive way that could serve both

Brazilian and American women came to me with the intention of going through a process of self-discovery through behavioral therapy, something I knew of. I began to understand the importance of this process and how it reflected in the way we dress, whether for doing business, having a company, or for those who were already working.

One day, I attended a lecture on entrepreneurship here in California. We had to present our businesses or ideas, and when I shared my proposal, I realized it was well received. However, every idea needs a foundation to be understood and embraced the way we want, and I still needed to possess the main element: security. People only buy into the idea of those who convey confidence, and no matter how creative I was, I did not convey what everyone desired: security.

Our authority comes from more than just the clothes we choose; for example, if you choose to wear a blazer and think that this single element will bring authority, you are mistaken. Or believe that choosing cool clothes, taking a picture, and doing the same pose you see on social media every day and thinking it will work for you will also not happen. Our authority does not come from being authoritarian. After all, that would show a lack of education. It comes from people who see you as a reference in your professional field, showing that you can influence people with your knowledge and skills.

How do you achieve this? How do you develop this security?

Every process requires patience, and your security will develop slowly, not overnight. My posture, the way I communicated, and how I walked externalized my insecurity. And how did I create it in such a short time? I had to look at myself and see that I had gone through the process of self-discovery and self-awareness. Let's see how:

One day, when I was looking at my social media, I saw a woman talking about how her mentoring would make a difference in developing our personal brand. I found it interesting and started paying attention, mainly when she spoke of branding, which was still new to me then. I just wanted to open a clothing store, but one that was different, and I needed to figure out how, where to start, or what to do; I was pretty lost, to be honest. So, she launched this mentoring program, and I decided to join, but without creating too many expectations.

In this mentoring program, I met Mila Moura. She changed my perspective on business and networking. In the mentoring sessions, she met with the students, and since I live far away, as soon as I purchased the mentoring, she immediately scheduled a coffee meeting. During our meeting, I mentioned that I felt insecure and was embarrassed to open Instagram and film myself. She started talking and told me about the importance of the digital world. I can't explain where the courage came from; I believe it was because I had support on my side, someone who wouldn't judge me if I didn't do it perfectly, so I opened Instagram and said:

"Hey, how are you all doing? I suddenly appeared with a new look—that's me! Out of the blue, I show up here. I had a very special coffee this afternoon with none other than Mila Moura."

It was a single video that once again pressed the courage button—that button that says, "Just go for it!"—but I wasn't sure if I could quickly overcome my shyness or if I would have the confidence to continue when I was alone.

What inspired me was that woman I connected with, who had stepped out of her comfort zone because simply moving to another country was just part of that process. She had left her secure public position, which provided her with a lot of security and financial stability, to do what she loved. She had studied for countless nights during shifts to become an authority in her field. After all, nothing happened over-night, and she knew where she wanted to go and planned and studied a lot, which gave me confidence.

I started the mentoring program—every Tuesday at 3 p.m. Even while still at work, I managed to watch all the clas-ses. In the first class, I needed to write my entire story, and at that moment, I was able to see what no one else would do for me, appreciate my story, and see what I had already achieved, which, in the eyes of others, did not make much of a difference.

Writing our story makes us realize how much we invest in ourselves. We often do not reflect on our motivations, even though they are fundamental to our development and positioning. It is essential to understand how we perceive ourselves, remember important points of our trajectory, and identify why we stopped doing certain things. Mila ad-dressed these aspects, and I needed to develop them at that moment.

So, all that knowledge I was gaining made me see my po-tential more and more each day and that I was on the right path. I knew why I was doing everything, which is an important point. Stop and ask yourself: Why am I doing this? Why am I heading down this path? Where do I want to go? Knowing these answers will make a total difference in your journey. They made a difference in my image.

Our security is a daily construction acquired over time. It was noticed when I posted videos on Instagram because people saw my progress, which resulted from all this external work. But was that enough? No, it was at that moment that I created an innovative and exclusive method of image consulting.

What is this method? Why does this method make a difference in image consulting?

Self-awareness leads to developing self-confidence in your self-image. So, knowing your story from another perspective and externalizing it helps you value yourself. Understanding how your personality works generates even more self-awareness. Dressing as yourself is a combination of harmony through your knowledge of yourself, your style, and the message you want to convey.

What outfit makes you feel unique, beautiful, and stunning?

_____

_____

Why does this outfit evoke these feelings in you?

_____

_____

It's challenging to let go of these clothes because they have marked special and important moments in your life, or have been part of an achievement, or simply because you wear them as people always mention how stunning you look, leading to a sense of confidence and value. You will certainly feel how much these compliments reflect on your self-esteem and even your mood. Compliments tend to validate our choices and contribute to a sense of self-confidence and well-being.

Have you ever noticed that when you're sad, you end up choosing clothes that don't seem to be flattering or make you look pretty, and surprisingly, it's on those days that people compliment you more? Why does this happen? There are some reasons related to our behaviors that can explain this. When we're sad, we tend to opt for pieces that make us feel comfortable, confident, and beautiful. This choice may be conscious, as we seek something that provides us with some emotional comfort. Additionally, these clothes can enhance our outer beauty and positively reflect our inner state.

When we're sad, wearing something that makes us feel good can transform our appearance. A particular outfit can highlight physical features and even improve our posture, making us feel and look more beautiful. After all, in those moments of sadness, we seek emotional comfort, personal expression, and even a form of visual transformation that makes us feel better. Do you understand the power of your image?

Are you the party crasher of your image?

A party crasher is someone who enters a place without being invited. How can this be related to your image? If you are projecting an image that is not yours or that does not reflect who you truly are, are you not becoming an intruder in your own image?

Sometimes, we may feel pressured to fit into certain standards or meet others' expectations. This pressure can lead us to adopt an unauthentic persona, as if we were wearing a mask to hide ourselves. However, this attempt to fit in may make us feel like intruders in our own lives, disconnected from our true identity.

Do not become a party crasher!

Have you embraced yourself? It is important to remember that each of us is unique, with our own experiences, values, and principles. Instead of trying to mold ourselves to fit in with others, why shouldn't we embrace who we genuinely are? This means having the courage to express our true essence, even if it means being different or misunderstood.

When we embrace our authenticity, we cultivate a sense of security with our own image and with who we truly are. When we feel comfortable in our skin and confident in our identity, we radiate a more powerful and genuine presence. This inner security that I initially lacked allows us to navigate life with more ease and acceptance. We know that we are deserving of love and respect, and this is reflected in all aspects of our lives, whether professional, personal, or in a romantic or friendship relationship.

Therefore, the next time you find yourself trying to fit into a mold that is not yours, remember that you don't need to be a gatecrasher in your own life. Instead, embrace your authenticity and allow yourself to be you. People will accept your true self and love your true image without fear.

"We will always have choices to make, and I chose to focus on helping women feel represented and authentic through their image."

Why is it so important to care about clothing?

Many people blend in with the crowd. Standing out comes at a high cost, and some people are not willing to pay to be noticed. Each of us has unique qualities that are solely ours, making us truly unique. The expressions reflected in our choices are our styles. While they may appear similar at first glance, each possesses unique nuances that set them apart from one another. We are the uniqueness in the midst of plurality. So why still care about clothing? Because it is the only thing capable of expressing your authenticity.

Furthermore, your image adds value in the eyes of others, and if they feel a deeper connection, genuine admiration, or even inspiration to be more authentic with themselves, it will automatically be associated with your service, what you do, or what you sell.

Therefore, it is crucial for you to cultivate assertive communication.

To help you understand better, I will share a situation that happened to me and will help illustrate the concept of assertive communication.

One day, I scheduled a meeting with my friend. However, when she replied that she was not available at that time, her manner of speaking left me quite upset. It may seem like a trivial situation, but it can easily happen within a company or when dealing with a client. My friend's tone of voice and how she responded deeply affected me. Instead of reacting impulsively, I chose to calm down and wait for the right moment to address what had upset me, carefully selecting the words I would use because the intention was not to hurt but to understand what had happened. What was the result of this approach? When I finally spoke with her, I was able to clearly express the points that had bothered me. Surprisingly, she not only understood my feelings but also appreciated how I communicated and handled the issue.

Where is assertive communication in this scenario? According to the *Human Solutions* website:

"In addition to the words spoken, the tone of voice, pace, and pauses play a significant role in how messages are perceived and interpreted. These subtle elements can add additional layers of meaning and emotion to communication. As a result, they can directly influence how messages are received. Employees feel more encouraged to express concerns and opinions through open and respectful dialogue. This not only prevents misunderstandings but also avoids minor disagreements from escalating into exhausting conflicts." (FRANÇA, Sullivan. October 25, 2023)

Thus, both verbal and visual expressions clearly and objectively convey essential points to those who listen and observe favorably. This can build confidence in your words, promoting the establishment of a strong relationship. As a natural consequence, that person may even become a client.

When you pay attention to what you wear, you can exude authority, earning appreciation and respect. As mentioned earlier, a simple choice does not automatically guarantee authority. However, by intentionally aligning your image with your competence – choosing clothes that project confidence and professionalism – you can convey an image of authority and competence. Even if your professional competency or amiability is evident, if your image does not reflect these qualities, you may not be perceived in the manner you desire. Therefore, you can alter people's perceptions by investing in your personal image and carefully selecting your clothes, colors, lines, shapes, hairstyles, and chosen fabrics. This is because your image is not just about your clothing but the harmonious ensemble presented.

Chapter 4
Take Action and Network

"Elegance is not about standing out,
but being remembered."

Giorgio Armani

Dress Yourself

It all started when it was still just child's play, and I set up my own school on the terrace of my house and invited the neighbors, who were younger than me, to teach them. At that moment, I didn't know what it meant to be an entrepreneur, and neither did our culture or our parents encourage us to have our own business from an early age, as it happens here in the United States, but now I realize that I was already in the market. I had my own pediatric clinic to attend to all my dolls, and I was a doctor, a salesperson, a cook, and many other professions we try while we are still young. But often, we are not encouraged by our parents. We are rooted in the concept of how difficult it is to be an entrepreneur, and they did not lie. But which profession does not face difficulties? Who do you know that started big? Even for those who inherited the company from their parents, there was always someone who went through a challenging process and left their mark on the company's history.

According to Lucilene Maria do Carmo (in an article for *Terra Empresas* called "Entrepreneurship: the profile of the entrepreneur and their longevity"), entrepreneurship means implementing ideas and creating one or more businesses.

When you create something, and people start consuming your product or service, they buy because you solved a problem or met a specific need, such as clothing, emotional, nutritional, self-expression, education, or entertainment, among others. But what if your image doesn't align with what you sell? Will they feel confident and return?

Viviane Williams

Selling a product is as important as making your customer come back and be consistent. Your image is the key differentiator in your post-sale. How many times have you built expectations about a product and been disappointed when you bought it? When I got married, I decided to preserve my bouquet with a company in Brazil. It was the most beautiful thing, but after a while, it started to mold, and I was very disappointed. However, when I contacted the company, they said: "No problem, we can fix this for you, don't worry." And they quickly resolved it, and now I have this accessory forever in my living room from such a special moment for me. Depending on how the person handles your problem, you will surely return, buy, and recommend the service to others when they need it.

Our image is not just about how we dress; it is also expressed in our behavior and attitudes. Being elegant is also expressed in how we treat others, whether they are our customers, employees, coworkers, or partners.

Entrepreneurship also helps us connect with other people. Often, we try to separate the person we are from the professional and the personal, our public self from the private. But when we are consistent in our attitudes and behaviors, it will help people feel they can trust us. This also gives us the opportunity to create more genuine and meaningful relationships. They will feel more connected and comfortable dealing with someone who is transparent and authentic in their interactions both online and offline.

Have you ever admired someone you follow on social media and had the opportunity to meet them in person, only to find out they were not the same person they appeared to be online? How did you feel? Perhaps frustrated that they were not who they seemed. Consistency between our personality, values, and behaviors creates an image of coherence and integrity. As the saying goes, "It takes a lifetime to build a name and only a few seconds to destroy it." If you try to force yourself to be someone or have a style that is not authentic to you, eventually, you won't be able to keep up the facade, and it will end up damaging your image even further - not to mention that of your business. When we don't have to create a different persona from who we are, we can express ourselves more clearly and assertively, which will contribute to our image in a positive way.

Our name is very important in building our business image when we are entrepreneurs. There are many factors within a company that make it a strong, powerful, and different brand in the market, but through our image, many people will be able to associate positive attributes whenever your business comes to their minds. Important factors include clear values and well-established purposes, offering quality in services and products, and always bringing innovation and creativity. The last one I will mention is fundamental: excellence in customer service, whether before, during, or after you provide your service or deliver the product. Your next sale to the same customer depends on how you treat them.

You chose to undertake this because you cared about your customers' needs, saw in your service a difference that could solve someone else's pain, or even felt that need and pain yourself.

When I decided to undertake it, I understood that my image consulting method would solve a woman's pain when she truly wanted to dress as herself. No woman can dress as someone she doesn't know and skip the personal development part as if she were just dressing someone who wouldn't be honest with herself, it would be like wearing a mask that prevents her from being truly honest with herself.

Incorporating body analysis into my consultancy makes it exclusive and innovative. Discovering your essence is the fundamental part of your clothing. You will dress in security and self-knowledge.

To undertake is to stimulate the 5 senses of human beings, providing a unique experience.

When people visit Disney, it is almost inevitable that they share their experiences, and they often mention the huge lines they face. However, what makes the Disney experience unique is how they approach these long waits. Instead of simply waiting passively, Disney turns the wait into an integral part of the attraction itself. There are themed environments along the queues, full of details and interactive elements that transport visitors into the story of the toy they are about to experience.

In addition, Disney also uses advanced technology, such as mobile apps and virtual queues, to optimize wait times and provide a smoother experience for visitors. These combined strategies make people less bothered by the lines, as they are completely immersed in the magic and fun of the park, even while waiting to enjoy the attractions.

And what is the result? Despite the price they pay for entry and additional expenses, people keep coming back to Disney. This unique experience provided is as memorable as it is exciting that, every day, 120,000 people (according to the blog "Vai pra Disney") are willing to pay the price to live and relive this enchanting moment.

Have you ever been to a place with a pleasant smell and kept coming back just because it created an emotional connection with you? That's what I'm talking about. Here in the United States, people always manage to have emotional, sensory, and emotional experiences, making the country so different and unique. What have you created for your customers?

Living here in California, I noticed that many people come from outside to see and know Hollywood, and many people make an effort to follow Oscar night. And what is this night so special about? Well, it's a moment to celebrate actors and actresses who dedicated themselves to learning and knowing new professions to give their best to their characters and turn them into great success in Hollywood.

Now, think about female entrepreneurs starting their businesses, do they start with a full team already in place? Often, she starts doing a little bit of everything, just like the actors at the Oscars. The only difference is that you don't win any awards just for starting, doing, and needing to learn a little bit of everything. So, thinking about that, I created a networking group where people can experience an Oscar night, but this one is focused on entrepreneurship and networking.

Upon entering the restaurant, they are greeted with a red carpet, interviewed to talk a little about their business, and served champagne. After all, it's a night of celebration. As each of the 4 talks begins, dinner is served, and at each stage, the chef explains each dish paired with wine. We have a photographer available so they can take pictures on this special day. Before closing the event, we award an Oscar to each woman who dedicates time and energy to her own business or who strives to be promoted in the company she works for. In a single night, we offer them a unique experience of feeling in Hollywood, making new contacts (the famous networking) with potential clients, having a gastronomic experience, and also learning to develop professionally through lectures with experts in body analysis, communication, branding, and personal image.

Women embody strength and resilience and are aware that they possess a powerful and unique image to undertake. They can arrive and stand out wherever they wish or change the course of their stories at any moment. In the past, the business world was predominantly dominated by men, but this scenario is constantly changing, with more women taking on leadership roles and contributing significantly to entrepreneurship and innovation.

According to an article by Hannah Wilson, published on the site br.investing.com, one in three global high-growth companies is led by women (GEM- Global Entrepreneurship Monitor). In 2021, there were approximately 13 million women-owned businesses in the United States, accounting for 42% of all businesses (National Association of Women Business Owners). Companies founded by women in the First Round Capital portfolio outperformed companies founded by men by 63%.

One of the main reasons women undertake entrepreneurship is to have financial freedom and, more importantly, to have more time to dedicate to their families.

The following is a statement from Marcela Barros, an entrepreneur who left a stable and secure job in the public sector to dedicate more of her time to her biggest love: her daughter. How did she face these new challenges? What was her new field of work?

Let's find out together:

I come from a humble family, raised by parents who worked hard from an early age, and that's how I learned to handle some responsibilities. One of them was taking care of the house and my sister while my parents worked; this experience was unique. It taught me valuable lessons about teamwork, sacrifice, and the true meaning of caregiving. When faced with the choice of what to study to start my professional career, I decided to study industrial chemistry at the technical school in Pernambuco, but soon realized that this was not my calling, I would not be happy. And that's when, with a strong desire to help and achieve financial independence, at 15 years old, I started working with my parents. At that time, they were opening a motorcycle parts store while also being employed. At that moment, more than ever, they needed my help. I remember very well receiving merchandise, checking invoices, registering products, and selling. All of that was a completely different sphere from the world of a regular 15-year-old girl. But yes, I had a strong will and commitment to make it work.

By the time I turned 18, the business was no longer there, but I continued working. This time, replacing my mother during her vacation as an administrative assistant at the company where she worked. It didn't take long; I was hired permanently, and after 3 years, I reached the position of administrative supervisor. But that was still not enough for what I dreamed of!!! Soon after, I was invited by a friend to participate in a selection process at a major pharmaceutical company as an accounting consultant. I jumped at the opportunity! Even though I knew the person to be hired would be responsible for the entire coast of Pernambuco, meaning a lot of traveling by car, I went for it. The big issue was that this was the first time I had driven out of town!

I had a driver's license but needed to gain experience on the roads. I took part in the selection and was hired! My motto has always been: "Even if I don't know how, if it has to be done, I will do it." And so began my greatest professional experience at 23 years old. Cimed was a dream; my eyes sparkled. A family-owned company with a unique identity focused on growth and expansion at a frenetic pace. In 10 years, it went from being the 36th to the 3rd largest pharmaceutical company in the country. I loved everything about it and felt a deep sense of belonging.

There were great professional references there, starting with the CEO, João Adibe, a salesman, and many other executives who managed me. I worked in major markets such as Pernambuco, Sergipe, Bahia, and Espírito Santo. But my maternal instinct spoke louder. I nurtured with great love the desire to be a mother, and in November 2020, I discovered I was pregnant. When I returned to work after maternity leave, the company invited me to also coordinate Rio de Janeiro since there was no major account client in Espírito Santo to support the cost center. I thought long and hard before making this decision, as my work was also a great love, and I felt fulfilled.

But my daughter was already a higher priority in my life. I would not be able to miss one of the most important phases of her life. That's when I decided not to be away from her. I made an agreement with the company I loved so much, and that had been part of my life for 10 years, to dedicate myself to the great and true love of my life. And now? I thought... I spent several nights thinking about what I would do with my life. Because, after all, for someone who had been working for 20 years, waking up without anything planned, and not knowing where to go is one of the strangest feelings in life. I asked myself: "What to do? What will be my purpose in life now?"

Even though I didn't have a full day nor a schedule to follow, I continued to wake up early and do my physical activities as always, at 5 AM. It was at that training place, in a CrossFit box, where I deposited all my anxiety and frustrations; it was where I renewed myself every day. It brought me such peace and such a good feeling that I started to want to encourage others to feel what I felt.

But I asked myself: "How am I going to do this?" And still, without answers, I began to analyze what my needs were within that environment. I realized that none of the clothing brands I used or the more affordable ones in the area fully met my needs. From the fit to the more traditionally rustic style used in CrossFit, I didn't feel truly beautiful; something was missing. I began to notice that CrossFit had already influenced the gym-going public, with shorts being a more intense part of weightlifting training, but the more modern, stylish, and neat style of the gym had not invaded the CrossFit box. After these analyses, I thought: "Why not?"

I could broaden my audience and meet the needs of many women in the CrossFit box. There was my business opportunity! I focused and studied a lot. There were several fabric tests and fitting tests, and I went through various manufacturing plants looking for the best service. It took 8 months of hard work until the first test production. But there were still other stages. And after the piece was ready, where would I sell it? Selling online might take longer to gain visibility; the cost would be higher in physical stores, street stores, or malls. How would I sell those pieces? How would I approach people?

So, again, inside the box, I thought: "If I'm already here, why not open my business right here?" At that moment, I was already sharing my project with some friends, and they loved the idea. I talked to the box owner, and he quickly bought into the idea and facilitated the realization of this new dream. I rented a room inside the box and set up a mini-store, and in the first month, I was surprised by the revenue. However, the plans didn't stop there; now, the website is under construction, and there are several other sales expansion plans. When I look back, I realize how I was able to take advantage of all moments in life, both the good and the most challenging, without losing sight of my essence and prioritizing what was valuable.

I learned that discipline and willpower are the greatest empowering forces for achieving dreams. Don't give up! We are constantly evolving. What was a dream 12 years ago, working in a large company and being a great executive, has passed, yet I was still able to be my best version by undertaking. I fulfilled another dream: I am the owner of my own business and have financial independence without compromising my values. I want to inspire women to become their best selves. Never stop. That's the secret!

- Marcela (Businesswoman)

Build professional bridges, do network!

To unravel the intriguing universe of networking, we need to understand the true meaning of network, which means "work network." When we talk about a network, what comes to mind? And what does that have to do with networking?

We are immersed in an interconnected world. Today, the word network transcends the simple notion of a professional network, intertwining with fascinating analogies, like a fishing net. Just as a master fisherman delicately weaves his net, casting it into the waters to catch fish, we, navigators of the professional scene, must build our own networks—true webs of relationships to seize opportunities.

The construction of a solid network is intertwined with our personal image. As we navigate through various personalities and exchange ideas and experiences, we shape others' perceptions of us. Just as a fisherman relies on the robustness of his net for a bountiful catch, we trust the solidity of our network to open doors and create opportunities.

In the context of networking, we are not just talking about a series of business contacts but about a complex web of human connections, experiences, and learning. Each node in a fishing net plays a vital role, just as each individual in our professional network can contribute to our growth and success. However, building and maintaining an effective network demands more than effort; it requires a strategic shift. We must be astute in our interactions, nurturing genuine relationships over time. This network is more than just a source of professional opportunities. It directly influences our personal image.

A well-crafted network reflects not only the quantity but also the quality of connections. Each person in our network is like a valuable piece in a complex puzzle that is our professional journey. Much like a skillful fishing net, this web of relationships can be the key to achieving our goals, forging fruitful collaborations, and overcoming challenges.

Therefore, just as a fisherman values their net quality to ensure a bountiful catch, we must prioritize building a solid network to enrich our career and, consequently, our image. By weaving meaningful relationships, we lay the foundation for personal and professional growth, building a network that will support our goals over time.

Viviane Williams

Amidst all this, we must remember the joy of talking to people, the first step to embarking on this networking journey. And we must deeply love what we do. This passion is the spark that ignites communication, making your authenticity shine even among thousands offering the same.

I remember the day I finally overcame my shyness. That achievement was a milestone that turned each message sent into a learning opportunity. Before, hesitation and fear of making mistakes prevented me from seeking new experiences, but by overcoming that barrier, I began to communicate confidently, without hesitations. Even when financial gains were scarce, I saw the value in interactions and the growth opportunities that arose.

Overcoming shyness did not bring immediate economic benefits but opened doors to valuable knowledge. Every conversation and every exchange of ideas was a chance to learn something new and grow. Focusing solely on numbers can close our eyes to the richness hidden in experiences. Often, it is easy to lose sight of the actual value of the lessons learned along the way.

Every person I met and every mentor who shared their wisdom contributed significantly to my personal and professional development.

I love interacting with people, which is the starting point for entering the networking world. And you, do you fall in love with what you do? It is essential to have a passion for your activity because by sharing your vision with others, you can express yourself authentically, leading people to be enchanted by your service or product, even if there is a crowd doing something similar. Remember, you are unique, and you need to value that authenticity.

Now, how can you overcome your shyness to make networking successful?

The first step is understanding that our shyness, often perceived as insecurity, can harm our business and image.

But you can think: "I don't know what to say."

What can you do? Do you know that friend to whom you openly share your thoughts and ideas? What kind of friend would that be? The truth is that people remember much more how they felt when talking to you. So, listen attentively to what they are saying.

You might also think: "People will find me boring."

What can you do? People will always have an opinion, whether you are shy or not. After all, you have already made a first impression on them. So, take advantage of the opportunity to be heard and let them know the amazing person you are. We tend to judge ourselves more harshly and demand more from ourselves than we do from others. When we act like this, we put ourselves in the wrong position. Or you are also judging people in the wrong way.

So, to overcome shyness when connecting with people, you need to stop comparing yourself to others. After all, you don't need to be like everyone else, and you can also develop new skills, such as communication. Now, let's move on to the second tip that can help you: be more observant. See how people who find it easy to connect are developing. What can you learn from them? How do they start a conversation? And how can you develop this skill?

Thus, you will notice that they start by asking questions, and this can be the third step for you to start developing your network. I was shy, but when I realized my desire was to make people understand the importance of personal image within my network, I gave eight presentations in Brazil and two here in California.

So, what is the purpose of networking?
- To create real connections
- Increase professional opportunities
- Gain visibility and credibility
- Personal and professional development
- Knowledge exchange
- Access to other training opportunities

How can we do good networking?
- Be a good listener
- Keep in regular contact
- Be aware and committed
- Understand that it is a two-way street

- Be proactive and open
- Build connections
- Have clear objectives
- Ask open-ended questions
- Stay updated

Chapter 5
Your Image Has Power

"Find out who you are and do it on purpose."

Dolly Parton

Dress Yourself

The long-awaited day of October 15, 2018, arrived, the moment scheduled for our first meeting. Yes, he was coming from California to meet me in Recife. It was the occasion when I would finally meet the person who would possibly become my future husband, although at that moment I was not entirely sure. I wished for him to have a good memory of me, for that image of me to be fixed in his mind as a special moment for both of us.

Of course, what truly matters is who we are internally, but our image, especially in that first moment, has a significant impact. When I talk about image, I'm not just referring to external beauty but rather the message that the image should convey at that moment. The goal was to make an impact that confirmed the coherence between the person he spoke to via video call and the person he would meet in person. After all, the first impression is crucial, not only in terms of aesthetics but also in relation to the authenticity and coherence of our image.

Days before, I had already thought about what to wear, yet I wasn't sure if he would like it or if I would also like our meeting. I styled my hair and did my nails, and, very nervously, while curling my hair into loose waves (as they bring romance, lightness, flexibility, and approachability), I burned my hand! I was upset because my perfectionism threw a tantrum of annoyance, as I didn't want to show my nervousness. But there wasn't much I could do, so I relaxed, smiled, and went with three friends to pick him up at the airport. We were late, but we were laughing, all with a lot of tension and curiosity about how that unique and memorable moment would be. And like all my friends, they couldn't stop asking me questions like "How are you feeling? Nervous? What are you thinking about? Do you already know what you'll say when you meet?" When we finally arrived at the airport in Recife, we ran to the arrival gate, and I waited for him to come.

When we looked at each other for the first time, I gave that smile that came to mind, "My God, what do I do now?" I calmly waited. I was wearing black pants and a silver blouse with off-the-shoulder sleeves that were, in a way, under-stated. My hair was parted in the middle, complemented with basic makeup and heels. When he arrived, he ran to hug me, and then we went to the food court to talk a bit. Soon after, my friends and I left him at the hotel; later, we met up with my family and had dinner at the restaurant. He had never told me his perception or what he thought of me the first time we met until years after we had been married. He told me that when he saw me, he was certain that I was the woman he wanted to marry. Yes, our image holds power linked to our behavior and communication, having the ability to attract or repel people if not in harmony.

In many instances, people will react to our image before even understanding how we are and function, which is why our image is powerful.

According to the article written by Giovanna Fischborn, "When Emotion Speaks Louder: Understand How the Brain's

Amygdala Works," published in *Correio Braziliense* in 2022, an emotion occurs in 0.25 seconds. By 0.50 seconds, it is possible to recognize that emotion and, within 1 second, decide it. The entire brain is engaged in this process, but there is a group of neurons, the brain's *amygdalae*, specifically linked to the issue, and they are part of the limbic system responsible for emotional responses. Known as the "emotional brain," it houses regulatory structures, including the amygdala, governing an individual's conduct and emotions. It is the system related to basic impulses and emotional behaviors. The amygdala is one of the most important structures in emotional responses related to human social behavior.

According to an article published in Faster Capital, "How does the brain processes information and emotions" (fastercapital.com), emotions play a significant role in decision-making. The amygdala, a part of the brain involved in emotion processing, can influence our choices by assigning emotional value to different options. Emotions can affect the way we perceive, process, and remember information, how we evaluate risks and rewards, and how we interact with other people. Emotions can also trigger physiological responses, such as changes in heart rate, blood pressure, and skin conductance, which neuromarketing tools can measure. For example, when we are happy, we tend to be more optimistic, creative, and generous, while when we are angry, we tend to be more impulsive, aggressive, and biased. Emotions can also influence our preferences and loyalty, as we tend to favor products, brands, and people that evoke positive emotions and avoid negative ones.

The information processing system can affect the emotional system by triggering associations, memories, and positive or negative expectations. The emotional system can affect the decision-making system, enhancing or impairing cognitive performance, judgment, or risk-taking. The decision-making system can affect the information processing and emotional systems, reinforcing or correcting beliefs, attitudes, or feelings.

That was how I brought many memories of accessibility to my husband, making him remember his dear and beloved mother, even though she and I are very different. When we relate to someone, we seek references from our parents. So, the image brought comfort and accessibility to him. That's why our image is so powerful.

When we look in the mirror and analyze our image, we have an opportunity to look inward and see how we can evolve as people. How we present ourselves is of the utmost importance for our lives and those we interact with.

Our image is like a band performing at an event. Imagine that only the singer will perform acapella all night long without the help of the musicians. You might not even be interested in going because it wouldn't be good, but a beautiful song is formed when the band and the singer come together. Harmony is needed for it to be good for the listeners, just like visually. Or we can improve: have you ever tried singing without having that talent? What would people usually say? "Do you like to sing?" You would say, "Yes!" Your friend would respond, "Hahaha, then go learn, friend." This means that we all need technique for each profession. The band needs the musicians, and you need an image consultant to understand what looks more harmonious in your visual. A single element won't make a difference in your appearance or achieve your desired goal.

There was something that really made me pay attention to my image and give importance: whenever I decided to get dressed up, Americans would compliment me, like, "You look beautiful! I love your blouse! I love your dress!" These and many other comments made me take care of myself and my appearance, so I started to care about looking beautiful.

Our image is capable of doing more than we imagine. It can bring people closer or push them away, increase or decrease our presence, hide us or make us stand out, protect us, or draw attention. The way we present ourselves to the world has a profound impact on how we are perceived and how we interact with each other. Regardless of the time, globalization, technology, or the advancement of the internet, do you know what we increasingly seek? Individuality!

Individuality refers to the unique and distinct characteristics of each person that set them apart from others, such as physical, emotional, and mental attributes, values, experiences, and personal choices. It is what makes human beings unique in their way of thinking, acting, feeling, and relating to the world around them.

How about taking a moment now to think about your individuality? With the fast-paced life and many obligations we have to fulfill, we often forget our authenticity or what makes us unique.

Take a moment and analyze:

What is your individuality?

What are the characteristics you believe to be unique to you?

Below, I've listed some qualities that can be considered good and bad, remembering that the perception of "good" or "bad" is subjective and can vary from person to person. The important thing is to recognize the complexity and individuality of each person. Mark whether you have this quality or need to develop it, then write how you could develop it.

1. Empathy:

Good ability to understand and share the feelings of others. How could you develop it?

_____

_____

2. Determination:

Persistence and focus on achieving goals, even in the face of challenges. How could you develop it?

_____

_____

3. Honesty:

Integrity and sincerity in your actions and communications. How could you develop it?

_____

_____

4. Creativity:

Ability to think innovatively and find original solutions. How could you develop it?

_____

_____

5. Resilience:

Ability to adapt and quickly recover in the face of adversities. How could you develop it?

_____

_____

6. Altruism:

Tendency to act for the benefit of others, showing generosity and compassion. How could you develop it?

_____

_____

7. Communication Skills:

Ability to express ideas clearly and effectively. How could you develop it?

_____

_____

8. Self-awareness:

Deep awareness and understanding of oneself, strengths, and limitations. How could you develop it?

_____

_____

9. Selfishness:

Tendency to prioritize one's own interests over others. How could you improve?

_____

_____

10. Impulsiveness:

Decision-making without fully considering the consequences. How could you improve?

_____

_____

11. Rigidity:

Lack of flexibility and resistance to changes or new ideas. How could you improve?

_____

_____

12. Arrogance:

An attitude of superiority and disdain towards others. How could you improve?

_____

_____

13. Lack of Empathy:

Inability or reluctance to understand the emotions of others. How could you improve?

_____

_____

14. Lack of Responsibility:

Refusal to take responsibility for the consequences of one's actions. How could you improve?

_____

_____

14. Ineffective Communication:

Difficulty expressing ideas clearly or listening to others. How could you improve?

_____

_____

It is important to remember that these are generalizations and that each person is unique, with an unparalleled combination of characteristics. The judgment of "good" or "bad" often depends on the context and specific circumstances in which these characteristics are expressed.

Identifying your individuality is important in a personal image because it not only creates an authentic representation of who you are but also contributes to a range of psychological, social, and emotional benefits. This does not mean following strict standards but rather celebrating and expressing what makes you a unique person. After all, your image has power! Never forget the amazing person you are!

Having the best image means being yourself.
Your best style is what reflects you.
Valuing your potential starts with you.
Dress, only if it's of yourself!

Chapter 6

Your Business or Corporate Image

"A businesswoman needs a successful blend
of design and practicality."

Donatella Versace

Every Sunday night or Monday morning, you ask yourself the same question: What am I going to wear to work? Why is it so difficult to find something to wear for work? Why do you never have anything? Or better yet, why are your clothes always wrinkled? Have you never explored your workpieces?

Our image needs to be intentional and strategic. We should not manipulate our image but rather understand what we want to convey. For example, what story have you been telling through your image? Every story has a narrative, and by choosing clothing, accessories, shoes, colors, hairlines, and fabric, we are describing or showing who we are to others. Being intentional is managing how you present yourself to the world.

Many people intentionally wear their gym clothes and complete some tasks before starting to work out. This action motivates them to engage in physical exercise. Similarly, our intentional image can have that effect when we look in the mirror and instantly see a beautiful reflection. This happens because all the choices we make regarding textures, fits, cuts, and colors directly influence that sensation. However, it is important to note that with the help of a professional, you will be able to make more informed choices.

Therefore, to convey this intentional image, it is important to analyze some key points:

- The objective you want to achieve, whether it is to get a new job, a promotion, build a new network of contacts, strengthen your networking, or simply dress authentically and more confidently.

♦ Considering the message you want to convey, reflect on the values you want to express, both through your appearance and your behavior.

When it comes to being intentional without manipulating the image, it is essential that this behavior and the message you want to convey are consistent so they are perceived clearly and effectively.

Developing an intentional personal image before creating a strategic image is crucial because it establishes a solid and authentic foundation for your image construction process. This initial approach allows you to get to know yourself better, understanding your preferences, values, strengths, and areas for improvement.

Furthermore, by incorporating body analysis into my image consulting method, you gain a deeper understanding of your personality traits, which strengthens your connection with your true self. This self-awareness foundation is essential for creating an authentic personal image that is aligned with who you really are.

Have you ever wished to be remembered for your image? Have you ever wondered how to be perceived? After understanding the importance of an intentional personal image, it is essential to develop a strategic personal image to achieve the desired professional goals. This strategy will not only influence consumer perception but also impact their purchasing decisions, whether related to your product or service.

Therefore, to convey this strategic image, it is important to analyze some key points:

To establish an effective strategic personal image, it is crucial to start by defining your target audience and deeply understanding their interests. The truth is that we can only truly connect with a specific audience when we share common interests, so understanding their needs, preferences, and values is crucial. When creating a strategic image, it is essential to maintain consistency and authenticity in all interactions, both online and offline. This means being the same person in videos as you are in person, ensuring coherence and honesty in who you are.

Another vital aspect of this strategy is ensuring that your 'yes' truly means 'yes.' This involves fulfilling promises made to customers or followers, significantly contributing to building trust and commitment, and demonstrating professionalism.

To maintain an intentional and strategic approach to your personal image, it is essential to follow a consistent code that continuously promotes positive outcomes. This means understanding that each context requires appropriate clothing choices. For example, it would be inappropriate to attend a wedding in a bikini, which would be considered highly disrespectful. In every environment we frequent, it is crucial to dress appropriately, show respect, and convey a positive and suitable image.

First, it is important to understand the importance of the dress code and what it is.

What is the Dress Code?

In Portuguese, this word means *código de vestimenta*. For example, when you go to a wedding, would you wear jeans and a blouse? Obviously not. I hope you never do that. But why? Because on that occasion, there is a dress code. To make it easier for you to always know how to dress, try to imagine how the party host will be dressed so it will be easier for you to base your dress code on that occasion.

Why is it important?

It is through the dress code that we convey the desired image to the market and to our clients. Therefore, it is important to emphasize that in the corporate environment, it is extremely important because the professional must override the individual, as they will reflect the company's image. This can strengthen the image that people have of your company and further strengthen your presence in the market. But, there are some types of dress codes that you should know.

Types of Attire in Companies

In some places, it is common for companies or employees themselves to prefer to wear uniforms, which is very helpful. But how can you make this uniform more refined?

For example, if your uniform is just a t-shirt or a polo shirt, you can bring more formal pieces into this look, such as tailored pieces, a third piece, a belt, and/or opt for more formal shoes, such as slingbacks or loafers. But if your uniform is more formal, you can enhance your aligned image by always keeping it clean and well-pressed. Your hair should always be well-groomed, makeup should be light, and nails clean; you can invest in accessories, even if small; this will bring more personality to your look.

It is always important that your attire aligns with the culture, values, and image of your company. And yes, there are different types of dress codes for each type of organizational profile.

Formal Classic

This dress code adopts a high level of formality and remains true to tradition to convey confidence and sophistication. It follows a conservative line, requiring attention to detail and the quality of clothing. This style is widely used by high-level executives, such as CEOs, to reflect professionalism and authority.

Contemporary Formal

It is an evolution of the classic style, influenced by modern trends but without abandoning formality. It incorporates comfort, individuality, and a touch of modernity, balancing elegance and comfort. In this dress code, there is room for personal expression while maintaining sophistication and professionalism intact.

Professional Casual

Known as "easy chic," it is elegant without being overly formal. It is ideal for companies with a more relaxed culture or for those specific days when you can wear jeans in a moderate and good-quality manner, for instance, when formal clothing is not required.

Professional Sporty

A more flexible dress code, which could be called business casual or smart casual, as the clothing is more casual, meaning the style of clothing falls between casual and formal. Ideal for companies with a more laid-back culture or for informal business events.

Very Informal

This is a dress code where formality is not a requirement, so it is more relaxed and casual. Women are allowed to express themselves in any way they wish, freely and without concern for clothing rules. However, this dress code raises an important question: where do you want to go? Remember that your image can positively impact and should reflect you.

Our competence needs to align with our appearance.
Our image needs to communicate what we desire.

The first impression brings some positive sensations and judgments based on the few seconds that they stare at you; they judge your social class, financial situation, personality, and level of success. This means that after this quick evaluation, a door can either open or close.

It is true that the corporate image is linked to competence and various skills that the individual presents, but it is important for them to have elegance. Yes, elegance has as its fundamental principles the use of good quality clothing, attention to detail in garment care, the cut, and structure, and avoiding excesses, both in patterns and accessories.

But we can mention that the highlight of elegance is also directed towards behavior. It is of no use to be dressed in high-quality pieces without having good behavior or manners. Elegance is the combination of behavior with your physical appearance. So, make sure to have good posture and use the correct body language.

How many times have you sat down and your back wasn't straight, unintentionally conveying insecurity without realizing it? Yes, our body also communicates messages, and having an upright posture will convey confidence, security, and respect. Making eye contact and controlling our hands helps to avoid showing nervousness or impatience.

How many times in a conversation with friends have you spoken too loudly, and someone asked you to speak more softly? Verbal communication is an important moment to convey our thoughts, ideas, creativity, and solutions, and this communication can be spoken or written. That's why it's important to pay attention to speaking neither too loudly nor softly. Like everything in life, we need to find balance, speak clearly and calmly, and not only speak but also be a good listener. It will be very polite on your part, and this applies not only to the company but also to meeting the needs of your client.

Do you know a problem I had and needed to learn and plan much better? Punctuality. This is taken very seriously here in the United States, and it shows disrespect to those waiting. So, be punctual. Elegance also requires knowing how to use utensils at the table and avoiding talking while chewing.

Being discreet, kind, considerate of others, avoiding any comments that may offend someone. It is very common today on social media for you to comment on what you think on someone else's profile, but if it's not your business and you want to be a more elegant person, then don't comment. Having empathy for others' feelings is not only elegant but shows that you have manners. This type of behavior can avoid many conflicts within the company.

Regardless of our dress code, from the most formal to the most informal, it is essential that our behavior is in harmony with our appearance.

The connection between behavior, appearance, and elegance is not recent. When we study history, we can see that this relationship dates back to earlier periods when there were no clear distinctions between social classes. Clothing and behavior were visual indicators that differentiated the rich from the poor. How many times have we come across movies in which the protagonist needs to adopt certain etiquette norms to be accepted in certain social circles?

Although the distinction in clothing has diminished in the business context, the importance of education and etiquette is still evident. The quality of clothes does not necessarily reflect the education of the people who wear them, and this can create misunderstandings in the perception of your image. In other words, the message they wish to convey may be interpreted differently.

Our corporate image is a deep reflection of the values we cultivate throughout our lives. Every choice and every action shape the perception that others have of us, our company, or the entity we represent. Trust is one of the most important pillars of this image. It is crucial not only to build trust with the people we interact with but also to uphold the trust they place in us and our ability to deliver exceptional results. In a world where time is a precious and often scarce resource, having a successful image means offering more than just a service or product: it means being a benchmark of integrity, quality, and commitment.

Excellence is a constant pursuit. We must be demanding of ourselves and the quality of the service we offer. Every detail matter, from the first contact to the completion of the service and post-service. It is these small differences that strengthen the customer's perception.

I recall my experience when I worked a few years ago at an airline where the importance of treating passengers well was constantly emphasized. I decided to internalize that I was taking care of people's dreams. Every check-in was an opportunity to provide a special experience, whether welcoming passengers with a smile or offering consolation to those going through difficult moments. This approach transformed not only the passengers' experience but also my own perception of work. Today, when I travel, I expect to find the same care and attention to detail, as I understand the impact it can have on my journey.

Unfortunately, we do not always find the level of service we expect. Even when employees are well-dressed and seemingly trained to provide the best service, something seems to be missing. This leads us to reflect on the importance of not only following a script but also genuinely caring about people and the quality of the service we provide.

Finally, it is essential to understand that success in our corporate image goes beyond numbers and profits. It is intrinsically linked to our positioning in the market, how we relate to customers, employees, and the community, and the image we have built over time. Our mission and vision should be more than just words in a strategic plan; they should be principles that guide every action and decision, reflecting and strengthening our corporate image.

How can a corporate image positively impact business? And how can these impacts lead to significant financial results? To illustrate these points practically, why not learn about the story of a woman who transitioned her career to become an entrepreneur and transformed her personal and corporate image, achieving remarkable success?

It's not just about knowing your style, it's about improving your image, as everything communicates, and aligning your image with your values and your business's mission creates a cohesive and authentic presence that resonates around you.

Now, we will read about Mila Moura's journey, a professional who left a stable career to venture into her dream of helping other women. Her story is an important example of how your image can help you succeed.

A story of intentional and strategic image, does it yield results?

I am Mila Moura, a former federal police officer who, after 15 years, left the public service to dedicate herself to the professional development of women. It's funny to think that being a police officer was my childhood dream. When I was 10 years old, during a school assignment where the teacher asked us to write what we wanted to be when we grew up, I expressed for the first time my desire to be a police officer. Perhaps that came to mind because my father was a police officer, and he was the only reference for success that I had. At 10 years old, we don't think or talk much about the future, so when I needed to write something about mine, that's what came to mind, "I want to be a police officer."

I say that the sentence written in childhood programmed my mind for what I would do from that day on, following my school routine and later academics with the goal of passing a public service exam. And so it was done, I studied Law, and at the age of 22, I passed my first exam to join the Federal Police. What followed was what I always wanted, years of professional fulfillment following my father's career and having the financial security that many people dream of. For 10 years, what I didn't imagine was that during this journey, I would discover myself as an entrepreneur, a woman completely passionate about creating, executing, and dreaming. I spent years working in the police force and, simultaneously, building something new, different, and much larger than what I was doing.

I didn't know how to name it, but what I started doing at that time was branding, and through it, I learned to position myself. My name, my reputation, my values, I developed and strengthened all of this empirically, but over time, I realized that there was a method to it, and the best part was that it was replicable.

The method that worked for me and allowed me to occupy prominent positions in different areas could also be executed by other women, and that's why, to teach these women how to position themselves, I requested resignation from my childhood dream in September 2022. I left the Federal Police, and gave up my financial stability to live as an entrepreneur that had been pulsating inside me for a long time. Over the 15 years of public service, I understood that more crucial than our achievements is our identity.

Regardless of the field we work in, public or private, whatever the niche, our name should always precede everything we do! When we shift the focus from what we do to who we are, we can accomplish anything; that's the magic of personal branding.

I experienced this firsthand, and the whole process of developing my brand started with changing my communication at its first level, visual communication. Early in the process, I understood that our communication is responsible for showcasing our value, and communication through image is the first way to "speak" who we are. I truly believe in the power of image; our visual capital should be used as a set of codes that express our potential, and by investing in that, I quickly managed to express an intentional change in who I was and how I was perceived.

It was not just the clothes that changed; my positioning as a relevant personal brand was based on an entire imagery identity that unfolded into other forms of communication, verbal and non-verbal. Our bodies also speak, and this communication needs to be aligned with the value we establish for our brand.

From everything I've lived and put into practice in my own story, I truly believe that every personal brand needs to master these 3 levels of communication to stand out. That's what I help women do, with self-awareness and managing how you present yourself to the world, it's impossible for a woman not to be noticed. I believe in this so much that I decided to transition my career at the age of 40 to teach women how to differentiate themselves through their personal brands.

Entrepreneurship is not easy, but living a life without purpose isn't either, so I chose the first challenge and am writing a new story with a lot of dedication. Today, one of my areas of expertise is as a personal brand manager. I teach women to build their personal brands through branding and then manage these brands through 3 pillars: Personal Image, Verbal Communication, and Non-Verbal Communication.

In my first year as an entrepreneur, I won the PIPE award in the Entrepreneurship category, an award provided by Diário de Pernambuco and agency Tero for digital influencers in specific categories. And in October 2023, I formalized my company, Grupo W, a group that had previously been hosting in-person events, but transitioned into a digital platform and became the first platform for female businesses in Pernambuco.

It is always a pleasure to talk about my journey and to honor the determined 10-year-old Mila Moura. She thought she wanted to be a police officer, but her determination showed that she could find fulfillment through entrepreneurship. And here we are!

Mila Moura - Entrepreneur

I - Imagine and be the person you want to be
M - Stand firm in your values
A - Hone your skills
G - Like who you are
E - Externalize your self-confidence
M - Improve for yourself

Chapter 7
Taking Care of Yourself

"Self-image is the essence of human personality
and behavior. Change the self-image,
and both will be transformed."

Maxwell Maltz

How about taking a moment to look at yourself? How about understanding that we, women, need to care for ourselves and love ourselves more than we usually do? You are so special and beautiful, regardless of the shape of your body, whether you feel a bit fuller or too thin. We don't have a standard to follow. We should feel good and comfortable with who we are and how we are taking care of ourselves.

You have seen in these chapters how essential it is to be involved in your appearance. But, hold on! We're not going to change overnight. You don't have to feel bad or sad because your relationship didn't work out, or if it's going very well and you're going through a tough phase, or if it's so good that you're afraid everything will change. You know, everything affects our feelings and everything changes who we are externally. So, what's the point of going through the whole process of external change if you forget the fundamental, which is to look at yourself?

Have you ever traveled alone? Have you tried spending time with yourself? Have you tried to see how pleasant your own company is? Having a moment to yourself is so precious! I had never done this before, and earlier this year, I had to travel alone for work. Exploring the world with yourself may seem lonely, but it's fantastic! Arriving at the hotel room, listening to your music, looking at yourself, getting ready, feeling beautiful, and then going out to do what you love the most, in my case, talking about image. Or better yet, have you ever tried going out with your friends, having wine, talking and laughing with each other, dancing, and feeling alive? Do you know why I'm saying this? Because we can never have a strong and powerful image if we don't nurture our most precious asset, our emotional well-being. It needs light and happy moments because, after all, not every day is like that.

Try to look at yourself more, play a song you love, light a scented candle, and take a bath that shows your care for yourself. No one will love you more than yourself. And yes, this care and love will naturally reflect in your image. I already know you'll tell me that you don't have time for this and would like to do it very much. The truth is that we only prioritize what is truly important in our weekly, monthly, and yearly planning.

Now I ask you, why aren't you in it? If you understand the importance of your image, I can now give you some tips on what you can avoid so that it doesn't have any interference. It usually happens with the hustle and bustle of daily life, and we start neglecting "simple" things, but even so, they can still harm your image.

When you choose not to take care of yourself, that can somehow harm your company or the company you work for and consequently affect your credibility. As the saying goes: "It takes a long time to build someone's trust and only a few seconds to destroy it." Taking into account what we have already discussed about the first impression, which is made in seconds, then you will agree with me that it is important to take care of yourself. The amount of knowledge you have about what you do and your company is as important as your image.

Image with and without visual noise

Here are some mistakes:

1- Low-cut clothing.

Instead of opting for a low-cut neckline, what you can do is wear a V-neck garment, which, in addition to elongating the neck area, will be more elegant when it never extends below the height of the armpit.

2- Too tight pieces.

Some women may think that their clothing fits properly, but it may compromise their look if it is extremely snug in a corporate environment. Seems like it can't get worse, right? In fact, depending on the fabric, it can even be embarrassing. So, remember that certain fabrcs are not recommended, such as: fine knits and viscose. These fabrics, aside from ac-centuating areas that don't need it, can pull, ride up, and cre-ate situations that may cause you to miss out on great op-portunities. I'm sure you don't want to give the impression that you were vacuum-sealed, do you? Therefore, opt for more structured fabrics that will enhance you and your body, while also conveying a much more positive message.

3- Dirty or messy hair.

You styled your hair on Sunday to look beautiful on Monday, and by Wednesday, or even earlier, it will undoubtedly be greasy, but in your mind, there are only two days left until Saturday, your day off, so you can wait. Actually, no! I hate to disappoint you. As crucial as choosing your outfit, the care of your hair is just as important; it is part of your personal image and needs your attention, as it can compromise the message you wish to convey. Do you know what message dirty and messy hair conveys? Negligence and carelessness. Is this the message you would like to transmit? I hope not.

But what can help you in these situations if you truly don't have time to wash it? A bun, ponytail? No, woman, I'm sure you've thought of that, right? The best option would be to have dry shampoo, as it can be a lifesaver and aid in your image.

4- Poorly maintained shoes.

Have you ever had a shoe peeling and thought that no one would notice? But nothing goes unnoticed, you know that, don't you? How about avoiding that? Well, it's worth mentioning that you want to achieve good results, and neglecting your shoes can also compromise your professional image, especially if your shoes are light-colored. Strive to be well put together from head to toe.

5- Scratched or cracked bags.

Your bag is an important accessory that will never, ever go unnoticed, causing what? A bad impression! Therefore, always remember that, just like your shoes, your bags complete the harmony of your image. This means they can either enhance your look or detract from your strategy. I'm not saying you have to buy expensive bags, but it is important to always have bags that can further enhance your image.

Consulting is like refined poetry.
It accentuates your curves, revealing the best of you.
True poetry lies in the neglected corners of your being,
freely reflected in your image.
Each strand of hair, sometimes clinging to your face,
silently bears witness to the tears shed in moments

of loneliness.
Poetry is present in your closet, filled with memories that
are yours alone.
You are a woman, a poem in its purest form, overflowing
with stories to share.
Your eyes, often smiling when they want to cry.
But your smile, oh, your smile is yet another curve you
hide behind the pain - just smile with your best curve.
True poetry is taking care of yourself.

Chapter 8

"My friend, I Have Nothing To Wear"

"The worst fashion faux pas is to look in the mirror and not see yourself."

Iris Apfel

Have you ever been invited by a friend to go somewhere and said, "I have nothing to wear, my friend!" Or, do you have a commitment and immediately think of an outfit, but when you try it on and look in the mirror, the unfortunate surprise: "I can't believe it doesn't look good!" Now you're having one of those days and have an important meeting. When you open your closet, you can't decide; nothing works, nothing looks good, not even those combinations you always wear, you just can't like anything.

Another situation: you need to go out, you've tried everything and nothing looks good. So, you put together an outfit that seems like the best option for the day. But when you arrive at your engagement, you receive many compliments, yet you can't feel beautiful. Can you imagine arriving at a store you love that happens to be having a huge sale, thinking it's your lucky day and you'll get several nice pieces? However, in your rush, you didn't try them on properly, bought multiple items, liked some, and others just sat there because you don't know how to wear them or why you bought them in the first place, feeling a bit lost and realizing you wasted money. Do you ever feel like that, sometimes, going on a shopping spree without really needing anything, making choices without knowing your closet well?

You've just ended a relationship, are getting married, or have landed a better job, and the first thing you think is, "I need clothes for this event, or I need to cut my hair for this new phase of life; a fresh start has arrived, and now I need a new look, to see myself differently, after all, I'm a new woman." Or perhaps you're simply tired of your appearance and want a change.

Right after the pandemic, on May 4, 2021, *Vogue* published an article about the significance of clothing on our mood. Hajo Adam and Adam D. Galinsky explain the phenomenon in their article "Enclothed Cognition," published in the Journal of Experimental Social Psychology in 2012. They affirm that clothing can influence an individual's biological processes, potentially altering mood, performance, behavior, and self-esteem.

When we think about going somewhere and consider what to wear, a series of questions arise, like, "What should I wear? How should I do my hair? What makeup should I apply? Should I wear gold or silver accessories or mix them?" Or, in a specific situation, have you ever been told, "Walk properly"? You may also hear, "But that's not in style." Then comes the famous phrase, "Friend, I have nothing to wear!"

Limiting beliefs occur when you have a closet full of clothes but still feel like you have nothing to wear. The underlying issue here is valuing quantity over quality and the right strategy when selecting an outfit. This mindset can result in impulse shopping and a disorganized appearance.

How can Image Consulting help you?

Studying what you want to achieve with your image. Mapping your personal style to understand your personality traits, so you can identify gaps in your closet and develop a new strategy considering your life style and budget. This approach allows you to buy what you truly need.

What is fashion?

FASHION - Derived from Latin - modus - which means ways or manner. There is a connection between these two words: fashion, referring to the way of dressing at a particular time; and modus, referring to the mode or way of doing something.

Is this in style? Are you fashionable? Or is this the latest trend?

There are many variations we find for such a small word with a powerful meaning and various nuances. Additionally, fashion has the power to influence our habits, lifestyles, and the places we frequent.

You'll surely relate fashion to rapid changes; if you take too long to buy something, it's already outdated, or if you get it immediately, you're preparing for the next release.

If it's in style, it's because it's new, and something has become old-fashioned. This doesn't only apply to clothes but also to preferences, architecture, objects, languages, ideas, arts, and more. Everything can be of the past, or better yet, out of fashion, like the use of corsets and bodices, worn during the 17th and 19th centuries but offered no comfort to women because the aim was to have a slim or "ideal" waist, according to the customs of that time, so they needed to be extremely tight. Due to the discomfort, they were eventually abandoned.

Another element of old-fashioned fashion that we've seen a lot in stories between 1837 and 1901 is mourning veils, which were part of the culture and etiquette. They were worn as part of the attire when in mourning, often covering the face along with black clothes, symbolizing the pain of that moment and showing respect for the deceased.

But, if we stop to think, fashion is a mode of expression. For example, in the past, people could distinguish between the rich and the poor based on their clothing. There was also a distinction between men's and women's clothing. Another example is the influence fashion had in the post-pandemic era and how we use our image today to express our desires quickly and directly. The way we dress expresses our competence aligned with the image we wish to portray, to achieve our financial results, or to connect with another individual.

Have you ever played "Pictionary"? Imagine that you can only draw to help your team guess the word, but your drawing is very poor, and your friends say every word except the one they should. This could happen when you try to wear what someone else wears or try to be something you're not;

people will interpret everything about you except what you desire.

Now, imagine the person playing manages to draw something very accurately, and everyone shouts the same word at once. Everyone is amazed at how skillful their friend is at quickly drawing something incredible. When asked how they did it, they say: "Oh, I practiced" or "I learned how to do it." We are not born with any skills; we need to develop them.

Beauty needs to be developed. It's normal to ask for your friend's help, but you shouldn't lack confidence in what you wear to the point where you always need her opinion to feel secure and beautiful.

One day, Tyler invited me to dinner. He always gave me advance notice, and the question always came to my mind: "What should I wear?" To make my situation more challenging, he never tells me where we're going; he just sends the invitation. If it's a fancier place, he suggests a dress; if not, he suggests I wear pants. So, this became a direction for the place we would be dining. But one day, as I picked out my outfit, I looked at myself and changed my top. He looked at me and said, "Sweetheart, I didn't like that change you made to your outfit." What do you think I did? Did I change back to please him? I could have put on the previous top, but my response was: "Sweetheart, just wait for me to finish." He looked at me when we left and said, "My love, you were right. It looks much better now."

Do you know what that day taught me? It taught me that, even though sometimes we may seek help or someone gives an opinion, I need to know and be confident that the outfit I chose is the right one. Of course, I can't be stubborn and never change; there needs to be a balance between what is truly beautiful and what is not. However, as a professional in image and style, I always ask myself before getting dressed: "What message do I want to convey?" It helps me make decisions when shopping and getting dressed.

Regarding change, it's important to mention that I've made comments like this: "My friend, I have nothing to wear because I've gained weight." Few things are as embarrassing as this statement. By expressing my vulnerability, I realized that people don't always understand the personal struggles I'm going through because they are often unaware of the emotional battles we face.

The first important point is that we need to respect someone else's body, and if your friend didn't ask for your opinion, just don't say anything. We are constantly changing and evolving. Many factors lead to an increase in weight, and unlike numbers, our self-esteem can plummet to the point where getting dressed becomes a significant barrier. These women try to hide their pain by wearing black, attempting to conceal a pain that only they carry, and often become the target of thoughtless, unfunny jokes, and in the darkness of sorrow, they cry as if the blame lies entirely with them. Usually, after pregnancy, when the body takes time to return to its previous state, anxieties, depression, or other disorders may arise, leading you to neglect yourself momentarily and fall into a difficult path to regain balance.

When I moved to California, all the suffering and use of medications accumulated and turned into stubborn pounds that are hard to get rid of, and worst of all, I don't enjoy physical exercise. I am aware of all the benefits and feel so good after I finish a session; I feel more energized, eat better, and often see the numbers on the scale decrease, but today, I understand that I should focus on my health instead, after all, it's part of my image and what I intend to project. Women, don't stop loving yourself and taking care of yourself; it's important to accept yourself and feel happy, but the best thing is to have good health to face all the daily challenges.

How does pregnancy impact changes in a woman's body? How does this reflect in her image? What changes concerning dressing?

I decided, along with my husband, that we didn't want to get pregnant, and this is also a burden we carry in society because it affects one's image and the way people see you. But what about women who decide to? What changes for them? I spoke with some women, and they shared their feelings.

"Vivi, during pregnancy, I was absolutely uninterested in vanity; I dressed haphazardly because all my focus was on getting the layette for João, the exams - I was a bit over-whelmed with everything. When he was born, I realized I was a woman again, and then I started working out and taking care of myself again (and the clothing issue came along). But it wasn't a decision to let go, you know? When I noticed, I had already let myself go. I just looked for clothes that fit me with no criteria. Many mothers took a while to see them-selves as women in the postpartum period. My problem was during pregnancy. I thought I looked BEAUTIFUL with 16 kg above my weight and *poorly dressed*. It's so crazy! When João was born, it clicked, you know?"

Nathalia Luna - Pharmaceutical industry manager

"It affected EVERYTHING! At the beginning of the first pregnancy was tough to understand the changes in the body, especially in the first three months, because you gain weight but the pregnancy isn't visible yet, and in the end, if you re-lax, you gain more weight than normal, then add fatigue and bad mood... It messes with self-esteem completely. In the beginning, it decreases, and in the end, it increases because you show more with the belly, and you feel the right to wear whatever you want, just focusing on comfort. I was 22 pounds overweight in Lara's first year. I gained 48 pounds during pregnancy. What an absurd! In the second pregnancy, I was more aware and gained only 19 pounds."

Roberta Monteiro - Hospital manager

"Everything changed. After becoming a mother, I couldn't see the person I was before getting pregnant in my new body. I couldn't wear the same clothes as before, and it wasn't just because they didn't fit anymore. I needed to choose clothes that made breastfeeding easier, that didn't highlight the belly as much (which is not the same as before), and the clothes needed to give me mobility to be able to take care of a child comfortably. Even today, my mind sees my body but can't assimilate that this is my new body. There's all that romantic part that says that the body you have today has brought life, that the belly was home, and the breasts nourished... That's true, but in practice, you still want to feel attractive and beautiful (something you didn't even know you were before). I don't believe (it's my point of view, maybe it's different for another woman) that the happiness of being a mother can influence my feelings about my body. They are separate things for me. Being a mother is wonderful. But it also has a more challenging side. And this side carries a great weight. But not everyone is ready to talk about it, as well as to listen. It seems that when a mother expresses herself and talks about the challenges, she's saying she doesn't like being a mother, or she regrets it, that she doesn't like her child. That's why most only talk about the good parts."

Eliz Muniz - Nurse

How long?
How long does it take you to get ready?
How long do you spend doing your makeup?
How often do you buy new clothes?
How much time do you dedicate to self-care?
The truth is, we plan so much, and many times, there needs to be more time, either due to the numerous things we need to do or simply because the right time has yet to come.

Nothing is good enough, is it?

For at least five days each month, women feel overwhelmed by premenstrual tension (PMS). The feeling is almost always the same: it seems like we never have anything to wear, and paradoxically, it's precisely during these moments that people compliment us, saying how "beautiful" we look. In these instances, all we really want is healthy or indulgent chocolate, a comfortable bed, and a good movie to calm the torrent of feelings and emotions that come and go in fractions of a second. Smiles, tears, anger, joy, and impatience arise and disappear so quickly that we don't even have time to relish or understand each feeling. We simply can't explain what all this is about.

Nothing seems to look good. Nothing seems right. We don't feel beautiful, and that outfit we usually wear on that specific day doesn't seem appropriate; something feels off.

Clothes are one of our forms of expression, and during these PMS days, they reflect the complexity of the emotions and internal experiences we are going through. PMS significantly affects our clothing choices, influenced by various emotional and physical factors:

- We prefer more comfortable clothes due to bloating and physical discomfort that are common during this period. So, we opt for looser pieces or soft fabrics. The physical comfort that the clothes bring is a priority to help us deal with emotional discomfort.

- Due to low self-esteem, we may not feel beautiful or attractive, leading us to choose clothes that cover more of the body or are less revealing, thus selecting clothing that allows us to feel secure.

- Emotionally overwhelmed, we simplify our lives by choosing simple and practical clothing to avoid additional pressure.

- When we experience irritability and mood swings, we may lean towards dark or neutral colors, while other women who decide to uplift their moods opt for brighter colors that make them feel better.

- Yes, we also become more sensitive, so certain fabrics and textures can be irritating and uncomfortable.

Despite this period being short, it impacts our decisions. But don't forget how resilient and powerful you are; you're just a woman to bear all these feelings and sensations. There's no playing the fragile sex card. We are incredibly strong to handle all of this.

Chapter 9

Psychoanalysis in Image Consulting

"The way you dress is an expression of your personality."

Alessandro Michele

Your Emotions, Your Best Friend or Worst Enemy

Written by Blenda Ribeiro

Racing heart, restless thoughts, a feeling that I have little time to do what I need, not finishing what I need? This option doesn't exist because peop e have expectations of me and who I represent to them, personally and professionally. They rely on me, so I have to go all the way without compromising on quality because that's my trademark. I strive for the best because I want the best; be ng demanding is necessary. However, what I fail to realize is that all of this is driven by fear, fear of being left behind, fear of being replaced, fear of being excluded, which is why I a ways want to give my best, to be desired, to be essential in the lives of those around me, always the chosen one. But how could I understand all of this?

Anxious heart, the urge to cry, feeling lonely even with many people around me, but it seems no one notices. It's written all over my face, and it's in my posture. Why don't they see? When I look at someone, I immediately perceive how they are feeling, but the same doesn't happen with me. What am I missing? I fail to see that the fear of abandonment makes me cling to everyone, including those toxic individuals who hurt me more than they heal me. I don't realize that I need care, yet I do everything to take care of others; all because of the fear of abandonment, the fear of being alone. But how could I understand all cf this?

I don't want to open up, I don't talk about my feelings, and I don't mix reason with emotion. Why is it so hard for people to be objective? Time is money, and my impression is that with each passing day, my efforts outweigh my salary. What am I not seeing right in front of my eyes? I don't see that it all boils down to my fear of being manipulated, that I fear being used, my weaknesses being leveraged against me, of being betrayed. But how can I be different? How can I act differently and feel good and secure?

Dreams

Big dreams exist within us, and almost perfect plans seem to unfold in our minds so that everything goes according to the script. On paper, everything goes beautifully well, but we forget that real life isn't a scripted movie; some monsters haunt our choices, ideas, and actions, paralyzing us; we can call them saboteurs. If you're not sure what I'm talking about, I'll give you some examples of the most common saboteurs. Ready for the list?

EMOTIONAL ENEMIES

The CRITIC:

It constantly leads you to find faults in yourself, others, and situations. It generates most of your anxiety, stress, anger, disappointment, and guilt. It lies to you that without it, you and others would become lazy and wouldn't get far. Many confuse this saboteur with their rational side.

The JUDGE:

A constant need for perfection, order, and organization taken too far. It makes you and others nervous and anxious, sucking your energy and that of those around you, making you frequently frustrated as things are never perfect enough.

The HELPER:

Forces you to seek acceptance and affection by constantly helping, pleasing, saving, or praising others. It causes you to lose sight of your own needs and encourages others to become dependent on you.

The VICTIM:

Wants you to feel emotional to gain attention and affection from others. It results in an extreme focus on internal, mainly painful, feelings. You waste your mental and emotional energy, and others feel frustrated, powerless, and guilty for never being able to make you happy for long.

The HYPER-RATIONAL:

It intensely focuses on the rational process of everything, including relationships in general. It makes you impatient with people's emotions, causing them to see you as cold, distant, and intellectually arrogant.

The HYPER-VIGILANT:

It brings intense and continuous anxiety about all the dangers surrounding you and everything that could go wrong. It causes tremendous stress that drains you and others.

The CONTROLLER:

An anxious need to be in control, control situations, and direct people's actions according to this saboteur's will. When this is impossible, you become anxious and impatient, leading people to resent you for a long time.

The AVOIDER:

Focuses on the positive and pleasure in an extreme way. It avoids difficult and unpleasant tasks and conflicts. It leads to procrastination and avoiding conflicts, resulting in explosions in conflicts that have been put aside.

But how would I know this, or how could I silence each of them in my head to be free and achieve my goals and biggest dreams? This toxicity that spreads and the negativity that, at many times, discourages me bring out my flaws, making me realize that I need comfort, Anxiety, overwhelming thoughts, and a sense of urgency to meet expectations. These feelings take over as I push myself to meet the high standards set by others. The pressure to consistently perform at my best and to never let anyone down drives me forward. But deep down, this constant need for perfection is fueled by fear of falling short, being replaced or left behind. Striving for excellence has become second nature to me, but at what cost?

As I navigate these internal struggles, I find myself grappling with a multitude of emotions, yet I struggle to express them. Loneliness creeps in despite being surrounded by others, and I yearn for connection and understanding. The fear of abandonment grips me, leading me to cling to toxic relationships that only worsen my inner turmoil. I fail to prioritize my own well-being, as the fear of isolation drives me to seek validation and approval from external sources. It's a vicious cycle that I can't seem to break.

I am constantly torn between the two in a world that values logic over emotion. Time is a commodity, and the relentless pursuit of success often leaves me feeling undervalued and overworked. Realizing that my efforts outweigh my rewards is a bitter pill to swallow. I struggle to strike a balance between work and self-care as the fear of being taken advantage of looms large.

In the midst of these emotional battles, I cling to my dreams, hoping for a sense of purpose and fulfillment. Yet, the road to success is fraught with obstacles and self-doubt, as my inner saboteurs threaten to derail me at every turn. The inner critic, the perfectionist, the people-pleaser – they lurk in the shadows, casting doubt on my abilities and clouding my judgment.

Viviane Williams

I strive to find clarity and peace within myself as I confront these emotional adversaries. It's a journey plagued with uncertainty and self-discovery, but I know facing my fears head-on is the key to unlocking my true potential. So, I take a deep breath, center myself, and bravely step forward into the unknown, ready to conquer whatever challenges lie ahead.

In a few days, I realized that my productivity didn't increase, my self-esteem didn't improve, and I didn't climb any steps on the ladder of dreams. That's when a turning point happened. The best decision was made: I hired an image consultant. The most important aspect was the professional I chose. I didn't opt for the first consultant I found on Instagram, Google, or TikTok; I chose someone who would teach me about the ideal attire and transform my outlook on the world, and that's precisely what happened.

Eager for the first meeting, my closet doors were already open, waiting for the transformation, just as I've seen on fashion shows. However, I was surprised to learn that my first meeting would be a consultation. A consultation? Yes, that's right. My first encounter was with a **behavioral therapist who specialized in Body Analysis.** But, of course, it makes complete sense. Transformation and care need to happen from the inside out; after all, everything must be based on my personality – not the one that is so prominent at this moment but my true personality. Now, everything has changed for the better.

In just one consultation, I was able to smile, cry, be enchanted, and be amazed by the profound knowledge I acquired in such a short time. For those like me who had never heard of body analysis, I brought all the information directly from the specialist who changed my emotional perspective on the world.

Body Analysis

Do you know when your personality started forming? What if I told you it was in your mother's womb? Would you believe it? Every human being is born with a 'blank notebook' where all the emotional stimuli that occur repeatedly in your childhood are noted. Have you noticed how children like repetitions? They repeat a song, a movie, or a clip thousands of times because children record and learn through repetition. Therefore, a brain record is formed if we experience the same emotional stimulus multiple times.

Now, I need to tell you an important point. Our photographic memory has not yet been formed from 0 to 3 years and four months.

Photographic memory? What is photographic memory?

Photographic memory, also known as eidetic memory, is a memorization mechanism. It involves the part of the brain responsible for registering images and turning them into memories that are stored or recalled whenever necessary.

Since it is formed over 4 years after your life begins, what happens during this period? All the emotional stimuli we experience, both positive and negative, go into the unconscious, which is responsible for our emotions. This is why a scent can make us feel good without understanding why; it probably stems from a time when your brain only recorded the emotion, not the image. Or we strongly identify with a piece of music but can't recall the reason; it's all stored in our unconscious.

Have you ever faced the following situation: a disagreement occurs between you and another person, and despite the conflict not being too intense or profound, your reaction of anger or frustration surprises everyone, including yourself? This happens because in each situation we face, our brain swiftly consults the unconscious to understand how we were taught to deal with a similar conflict, specifically during infancy from conception until age 5. This is why controlling emotions is sometimes challenging; these reactions are more linked to your past than your present.

What is the relationship between our personality, formed from 0 to 5 years, and the shape of our body (bone structure)? It is during this period that our bone structure is also being formed. Our unconscious shapes the developmental stimuli we receive, allowing body analysis to recognize our true personality, our abilities, needs, and fears—fears that may be guiding our actions and bringing us many negative feelings.

Why is body analysis so critical? Unfortunately, humans tend to believe that their own personality (way of acting, speaking, and thinking) is the correct way to deal with situations, often imposing that others change their behavior to please them.

Think back to every phase of your life. How was your school period? Were people trying to shape or change your childish way of being in that environment? And at home, did any family member try to tell or convince you that their way of thinking and acting was correct? Some phrases clearly show when this happens. Let's look at some examples:

- You speak too loudly. Speak more quietly!
- Stop crying! Or I will give you real reasons to cry.
- Get to the point! You take too many detours when telling a story.
- Stop being shy, child! Hug your aunt, who is greeting you.

These 'adjustments' in how we speak, think, and act distance us from our original personality, the one we formed in childhood due to the need for adaptation or survival. This situation can occur so many times that we may completely lose ourselves, leading to significant consequences in youth and adulthood, such as making misguided choices in professions and careers.

Do you know someone who started a course and decided to abandon it near the end? Or finished the course but never worked in that field? Or even worked in the field and realized a few years later that the profession does not bring happiness?

Do the consequences stop there? Unfortunately, no! The distancing from your original personality may lead you to choose a spouse incorrectly, someone who fulfills the needs imposed on you by others. Furthermore, there are past events that you may not be aware of, like a trauma your grandmother experienced that affected how she raised your mother, which changed your mother's perspective on your future, all of which, if not realized, will shape your choices based on fears or, worse, traumas that are not yours.

We can compare it to a Ferrari being put on a dirt road. Will it reach its destination? Probably, but because it was not designed for such terrain, what will its condition be when it arrives? How long will it take to reach the final point? Now, what if we put that Ferrari in the right place, on a super smooth track? Will the result be better? Absolutely, because the environment favors it.

In what environment have you chosen to be in?

But Blenda, can I not abandon my home, the environment I live in? Those who think I'm talking about a physical environment are mistaken. In what mental environment do you place yourself? In what emotional environment do you choose to dwell? Whom do you choose to inhabit your emotional environment? Who do you choose to share your desires, abilities, and concerns with? If you've never stopped to think about this, pay attention! You probably don't filter who comes in and out or exerts influence on your thoughts, actions, and emotions.

Many come to my office with ready answers to questions like:

- Why do you still have this life?
- Why are you still in this job?
- Why don't you change?

The ready answers are always: "But Blenda, you don't know my husband... Blenda, you say that because you're not in my daily life... If you had my life, you would understand."

What would your answer be to me? Write below:

_____

_____

Any sentence about your life that comes after an emotional change advice is an excuse, a justification for not making the change. Emotional change is a controversial topic among people because many believe it aims to revert to their original personality, which could result in distancing from the people their fears have chosen, giving you the (wrong) feeling of abandoning others.

Many people pay for coaching, performance feedback, therapy, workshops, and nutritional consultations in search of change, but soon all willpower fades away, and the desired result is not achieved. Even though they truly believe they want to change, there is great resistance to change.

This need for change comes from the desire to be happy. How much have you pursued this feeling? How many videos have you watched, how many courses or books have you read to be more productive at work or to be more organized in your daily life to feel happier and more fulfilled? How many times have you visited a nutritionist or followed that influencer who has a body shape similar to yours, so you believe that their 'diet' will also work for you? Have you achieved this or another goal? How long did the happiness last when you reached that goal? Why is it so hard to make these changes? And if you do achieve them, why is it so hard to maintain that state of satisfaction?

The answer lies in the enemies. Remember them? I described eight internal enemies that keep you far from reaching your goals, dreams, and satisfaction. Your goal should be to discover who your enemies are. Being aware of them is very important because it weakens them. Imagine them as thieves, always strong and stealing any improvements you try to make.

Let's do an exercise. Go back a few pages, analyze each of them, and find out who your enemies are. Write them down in order from the strongest in your mind.

Dress Yourself

1_____

_____

_____

_____

_____

2_____

_____

_____

_____

_____

3_____

_____

_____

_____

_____

4_____

_____

_____

_____

_____

Now, below, describe the consequences that each enemy has brought to your life, what you have missed doing, what kind of relationships you have missed having, and what dream you have left behind because of each enemy.

1st Enemy: _____

Consequences of it:

_____

_____

_____

2nd Enemy: _____

Consequences of it:

_____

_____

_____

3rd Enemy: _____

Consequences of it:

_____

_____

_____

4th Enemy: _____

Consequences of it:

_____

_____

_____

In the office, I always explain to patients the importance of stepping out of autopilot and into consciousness. What's the difference?

Autopilot:

Doing things on autopilot means performing tasks without really paying attention to them or consciously thinking about what is being done. It's as if you're acting mechanically, without emotional or mental involvement. This can happen when we're distracted, bored, stressed, or simply when something becomes so routine that it no longer requires our conscious attention. Examples:

- Driving to a familiar destinat on without exactly remembering the route taken.
- Reading a book or article without absorbing the content because the mind is distracted.
- Cooking a recipe you make repeatedly without really thinking about the steps or ingredients.
- Automatically responding "fine" when someone asks how you are without reflecting on your emotional state.

- Typing text messages or emails without really thinking about what is being written.
- Eating without savoring the food, simply swallowing it while doing other activities.
- Exercising mechanically, without really paying attention to the technique or body sensation.
- Watching TV without engaging in the plot or characters - just as a way to pass the time.
- Performing household tasks like folding laundry or washing dishes without really paying attention to the process.

Consciousness:

Doing things consciously means performing tasks with full awareness and attention in the present moment. Instead of acting on autopilot, you are fully present and engaged in the activity you are doing. This involves being aware of your thoughts, emotions, physical sensations, and the environment around you while performing the task. When you do things consciously, you are more attentive to details, enjoy the experience more, and can even improve your performance. Examples:

- Walking outdoors, paying attention to the sounds, smells, and physical sensations of the environment around you.
- Doing household activities, like washing dishes, and paying attention to what you are doing.

- Having a meaningful conversation with someone, listening attentively to what the person is saying, and responding genuinely and reflectively.

- Being mindful during meals, focusing on the eating experience, from chewing to the taste and texture of food.

- Writing in a journal, reflecting on the day's events, thoughts, and emotions.

- Appreciating a piece of art in a museum, observing the details, colors, and emotions it evokes.

Being conscious allows you to ask fundamental questions that prevent emotional outbursts:

- Why am I feeling this way?

- What will the other person understand from my words?

- Did the other person really mean what I understood?

- Is the way I received the other person's words in line with their personality, or could it be my traumas changing the meaning and context of the situation?

It is at this moment that emotional intelligence begins to act in you! Imagine a battlefield: on one side, your *emotional enemies*, who are strengthened by being on *autopilot*; on the other, your *emotional intelligence*, which is strengthened by your conscious mode, fighting off these thieves of positive feelings. The mode that will win is the one you use the most. In biological terms, these two modes act in different brain parts, which means that strengthening one weakens the other.

Who has more strength in your emotional environment today, your emotional enemies (autopilot) or your emotional intelligence (conscious)? Answer below:

_____

_____

_____

How are these enemies formed? Through the traumas and fears that have been passed down from generation to generation through autopilot, these difficult situations in life create negative thoughts that form mental patterns, habits, and beliefs based on fear, always seeking to be on high alert, as these enemies believe that positive feelings leave you relaxed (UNPROTECTED). In contrast, negative ones will always keep you on alert, ready to defend yourself as needed. Derived from imperfection, every human has emotional enemies linked to the need for survival, based on worst-case scenarios; the suffering endured by all humanity, from generation to generation, is your brain always expecting the worst.

The most important thing to know is that your emotional enemies derive from lies. How so? They all stem from future fears. What is a future fear, and what are its symptoms? A feeling of anxiety, nervousness, restlessness, muscle tension, and even panic about something that might happen but isn't happening.

What is your goal? Strengthen your emotional intelligence. How to do this?

Stepping out of autopilot and practicing awareness can bring a sense of satisfaction, a greater connection to the present, and certainly improve your relationships. Let's practice. Here are some activities that can help you step out of autopilot and cultivate mindfulness:

◆ Breathing exercises: Practice conscious breathing exercises, like deep abdominal breathing, to help bring your mind into consciousness.

Deep abdominal breathing, also known as diaphragmatic breathing, is a breathing technique that involves using the diaphragm, a muscle located below the lungs. This technique allows you to breathe more efficiently, maximizing the amount of air entering the lungs and providing a series of benefits for the body, and primarily for the mind, exercising emotional intelligence.

Here is a simple step-by-step guide to practicing deep abdominal breathing. You will do this every morning as soon as you wake up.

Let's go.

◆ **Posture:** Sit or lie down comfortably in a relaxed position. Keep your spine upright but not rigid and your shoulders relaxed.

◆ **Hands:** Place one hand on your chest and the other on your abdomen, just below the lower ribs. This will help you notice the movement of your abdomen during breathing.

- **Inhalation:** Breathe deeply through your nose, allowing the air to first fill your abdomen and then your lungs. As you inhale, feel your abdomen expand, gently pushing your hand out as you breathe. Imagine you are inflating a balloon in your belly.

- **Exhalation:** Slowly exhale through your nose or mouth, first emptying the air from your lungs and then allowing your abdomen to gently contract inwards. Slightly tighten your abdominal muscles as you exhale, pushing the air out as if you are deflating a balloon in your belly.

- **Rhythm:** Maintain a smooth and steady breathing rhythm without excessive effort. Deep abdominal breathing should be relaxing and natural.

- **Duration:** Try practicing for 3 minutes daily, gradually increasing as you feel more comfortable with the technique.

Practicing deep abdominal breathing regularly can help reduce stress, increase body oxygenation, calm the mind, and improve overall respiratory health.

In addition to breathing, one must have daily habits to help keep the brain in consciousness. I'll give you two key teachings to carry with you for your entire life.

Below, you will find some of these habits, analyze them, and write immediately after if you practice this activity. If you do, describe how you do it and compare it with the proposed ideal; if you don't, describe what you will do to include this activity in your week.

Mindful eating: Dedicate a moment to eat without distractions, no TV on, no radio or reading, completely focused on the experience of tasting and enjoying the food.

Do I practice this habit? ( ) YES ( ) NO

What will I do to include this activity in my week:

_____

_____

_____

Nature observation: Spend some time outdoors observing the nature around you. Observe the trees, birds, flowers, and other forms of life, and connect with the natural environment.

Do I practice this habit? ( ) YES ( ) NO

What will I do to include this activity in my week:

_____

_____

_____

Creative arts: Engage in an art form you enjoy, such as painting, drawing, sculpture, music, or writing, and fully immerse yourself in creative expression.

Do I practice this habit? ( ) YES ( ) NO

What will I do to include this activity in my week:

_____

_____

_____

Mindful walking: Take a mindful walk, paying attention to your steps, breathing, and body sensations as you move.

Do I practice this habit? ( ) YES ( ) NO

What will I do to include this activity in my week:

_____

_____

_____

Active listening: Practice active listening during conversations, listening with full attention to what the other person is saying, without thinking about what to say next.

Do I practice this habit? ( ) YES ( ) NO

What will I do to include this activity in my week:

_____

_____

_____

Conscious stretching: Practice conscious stretching, focusing on the sensation of stretching in each part of the body as you move.

Do I practice this habit? ( ) YES ( ) NO

What will I do to include this activity in my week:

_____

_____

_____

Observation exercises: Observe details around you that often go unnoticed, such as the texture of a wall, cloud patterns, or sounds around you.

Do I practice this habit? ( ) YES ( ) NO

What will I do to include this activity in my week:

_____

_____

_____

The second teaching involves the circadian rhythm.

The circadian rhythm is a biological cycle of approximately 24 hours that influences various physiological, behavioral, and biochemical processes in humans.

These activities will activate the part of your brain responsible for cultivating mindfulness and will help you step out of autopilot, bringing more awareness and presence to everyday life.

The internal biological clock primarily controls the circadian rhythm. This internal clock is mainly synchronized with environmental cycles such as sunlight but is also influenced by other factors such as temperature, physical activity, and sleep-wake patterns.

Some of the biological processes that follow a circadian rhythm include:

Sleep-wake cycle: The circadian rhythm regulates the sleep-wake pattern, determining when we feel most alert and when we feel sleepy throughout the day.

Wakefulness: It is the period when we are awake and conscious. During wakefulness, we engage in daily activities such as work, study, socializing, and performing daily tasks.

Sleep: It is the period when we are unconscious and resting. During sleep, our body goes through different stages, including light sleep, deep sleep, and the REM (rapid eye movement) stage, associated with vivid dreams.

Hormonal regulation: Hormones like cortisol, melatonin, insulin, and growth hormone follow a circadian rhythm, affecting functions like metabolism, stress response, and sleep regulation.

Body temperature: Body temperature follows a circadian pattern, peaking during the day and decreasing at night, affecting the sleep-wake cycle.

Brain activity: Brain function, including brain wave patterns and cognitive activity, varies throughout the circadian cycle, influencing concentration, memory, and mental performance.

Feeding patterns: The circadian rhythm influences appetite regulation and nutrient metabolism, affecting when we feel hungry and full.

The interaction between the internal circadian rhythm and environmental cycles is crucial for maintaining overall health and well-being, and disruption in the circadian rhythm can lead to sleep disorders, health issues, and negative impacts on cognitive and metabolic function.

Let's put it into practice. Fill in this image what your daily routine is like:

Viviane Williams

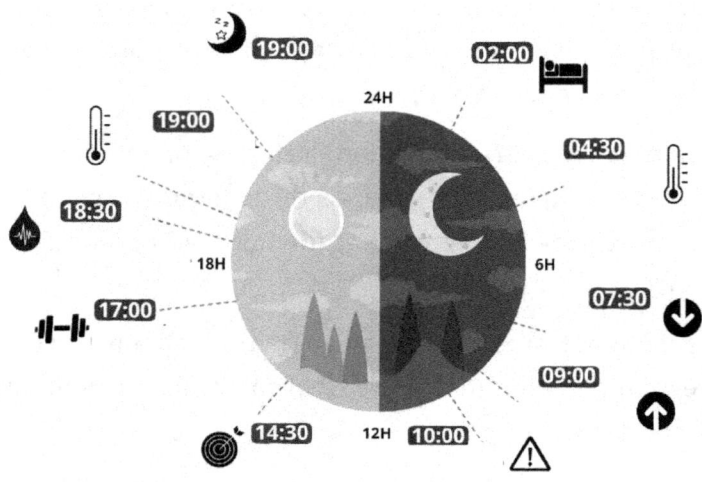

Circadian Rhythm

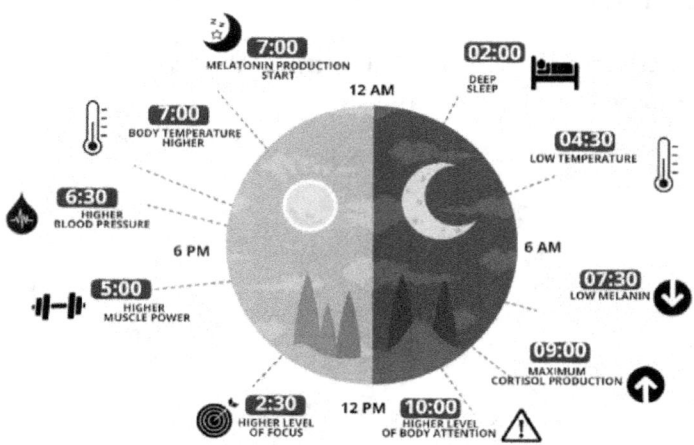

Now, you will fill in how you can adapt your routine to the circadian rhythm:

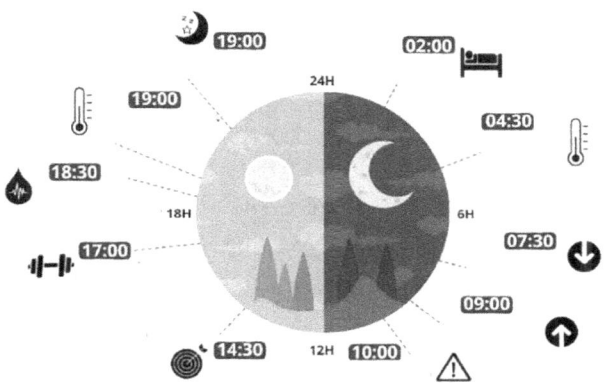

This is the goal of body analysis: to bring balance between your emotions, your dreams, and your personality. Having a routine based on the circadian rhythm brings a series of benefits to your health and productivity. Such as:

Better sleep quality: By following a routine that respects the natural rhythms of the circadian cycle, you are more likely to have deeper, more restorative, and higher-quality sleep. This can result in more energy during the day, improving mood and concentration.

Hormonal regulation: The circadian rhythm is crucial in regulating important hormones like melatonin and cortisol. A routine aligned with the circadian cycle can promote healthy levels of these hormones, benefiting sleep, metabolism, mood, and the immune system.

Better metabolic health: Studies show that following a routine that respects the circadian cycle is associated with a lower risk of obesity, type 2 diabetes, and other metabolic problems. This is because the circadian cycle influences appetite regulation, nutrient metabolism, and insulin sensitivity.

Enhanced cognitive performance: A routine that respects the circadian cycle can improve cognitive performance, including memory, concentration, decision-making, and problem-solving skills. This is because the circadian rhythm influences brain activity and brain wave patterns.

Greater resilience to diseases: A healthy routine based on the circadian cycle can strengthen the immune system and increase the body's ability to fight infections and diseases. This is because adequate sleep and hormonal regulation promoted by the circadian cycle are essential for immune health.

Better mood and emotional well-being: A consistent routine based on the circadian cycle can help reduce stress, anxiety, and depression, promoting a healthy balance between activity and rest.

Following a routine that respects the circadian cycle can improve various aspects of physical, mental, and emotional health, promoting a more balanced and fulfilling lifestyle.

Comparisons Moment

Now that you know your emotional journey within the consultancy, let's understand the difference between Personal Image Mentoring/Consultancy and **Viviane Williams' Mentoring.**

Personal Image Consultancy (standard):

- Personal style analysis
- Physical type analysis
- Wardrobe cleaning
- Personalized shopping
- Assembly of looks

Personal Image Consultancy Viviane Williams:

- Therapeutic Service in Body Analysis
- Emotional profile analysis + physical type analysis for style fit
- Interview with consultant Viviane Williams
- *Wardrobe* Analysis
- Application of garment combination guidelines
- Personalized shopping
- Assembly of looks

The difference in services and results is clear! The goal is not just to teach how to have a smart closet but to undergo a life transformation—a self-esteem transformation that starts from the inside out so you can apply the acquired teachings to the smallest details and throughout your life.

See you in our next session!

Chapter 10
How to Impress?

"It's not about appearance, it's about essence.
It's not about money, it's about education.
It's not about clothes, it's about class."

Coco Chanel

When getting married, it's natural to want to impress your partner. With so many new things, changes, and adaptations, it can sometimes feel challenging to maintain the impression we would like. At first, I confess I felt overwhelmed by the avalanche of emotions overflowing in my heart. But deep down, I was impressed by the strength of the love that united us.

Life in another country brought unexpected challenges. There were pains we couldn't share in words but expressed through my appearance and gestures.

I remember a particular night when my husband came home from work and found me lying down, struggling with the longing that squeezed my heart. Amidst tears, he started a very affectionate dialogue:

- Husband: How are you?
- Viviane: I don't know how to explain... I miss you so much. Today has been challenging!
- Husband: How can I help you?
- Viviane: I don't know. I just want to stay in bed, lying down...
- Husband: No, get dressed and come with me.
- Viviane: I'm not in the mood to go out. I just want to stay still...
- Husband: You'll like it, come on! Please!
- Viviane: I don't want to dress up...
- Husband: It's okay!

Despite being reluctant, I decided to get ready. I took a shower, washed my hair, and chose a simple outfit that reflected my feelings: a black sweater with pearls, black riding pants, and white shoes without a hint of makeup. In that appearance, all the pain of missing him was evident.

And so, we went to play golf together. During the game, I found a way to have fun and distract myself from worries. By the end of the night, I realized that impressing my husband at that moment wasn't about physical appearance but about our ability to support each other and share moments of joy, even in difficult times. According to the Oxford Languages dictionary, impress means "to cause or receive a psychological impression; to shake, move, cause or receive an impression in the senses; to attract attention or have attention caught by."

True impressiveness goes beyond the surface and lies in emotional connection. In our relationship, I learned that sharing our worries and emotions builds a bridge of understanding and mutual support. By expressing my anxieties and the longing that consumed me, I found comfort in my husband's empathy. This sincere exchange further strengthened our emotional bond, showing that being truly understood and supported by your partner is essential for the growth and stability of our relationship.

During a challenging night, my husband showed a deep understanding of my emotions. Even when reluctant to leave the house, he offered me his unconditional support, creating a safe space for me to express my concerns. His genuine empathy and compassion were crucial in strengthening our connection and reinforcing trust in our relationship. I learned that the ability to empathize and offer emotional support is essential for nurturing a healthy and lasting relationship.

How many times has your father, mother, friend, colleague, or another loved one needed you and had a good impression of you? How have you built your image based on these impressions or actions? And how has communication affected the way you relate to people? How do the people around you describe your communication? Our image and impression are built on our values, which are reinforced daily.

Causing an impression with our image and communication and achieving positive results in relationships is fundamental, whether with our spouses, friends, family, clients, partners, or any other person we interact with. The way we present ourselves visually reflects not only our personal aesthetics but also our confidence and respect for ourselves and others. Clear, empathetic, and assertive communication is essential for establishing meaningful connections and building solid relationships based on mutual understanding and trust.

Imagine walking into a room and being greeted with a warm smile and a firm handshake. That first impression says a lot about you and can influence how people see you. So, how we dress, our posture, and our body language communicate subtle messages about our confidence, professionalism, and even our personality.

On March 5th, we were in Las Vegas. The night promised to be memorable, as it was my first contact with my husband's family, and my friends accompanied me on this trip. He seemed nervous, which made me curious. As we headed to the restroom of the Top of the World restaurant, with its stunning view of Las Vegas, I was surprised. Tyler took my arm, knelt down, and proposed to me with a beautiful diamond ring. Every woman dreams of receiving a unique piece of jewelry, especially from someone who always seeks to impress. It was a unique and exciting moment!

I was thrilled with this delicate gift that impresses everyone wherever I go due to the uniqueness of the ring and diamond. All women aspire to impress, whether through resilience, strength in facing challenges, or through image. In my image consultancy, I recognize the unique value that each person carries, comparable to that of a precious gem. Let's explore this process together.

Imagine yourself in front of a rough emerald, a precious stone hidden beneath the layers of earth and rock. The rough stone can be seen as a metaphor for a woman in her initial state, representing her raw and unique essence, yet to be revealed to the world. Just as this stone holds hidden wealth within its layers, a woman carries within herself a treasure trove of qualities, talents, and potentials yet to be explored. The cutting of the stone can be compared to a woman's personal development and self-discovery.

Now imagine a skilled artisan specialized in revealing the true essence of each stone. So, she holds the rough emerald in her hands, carefully studying every detail, identifying each hidden facet, every nuance of color, lines, style, and every trace of its uniqueness. This artisan represents me, an expert in self-expression and authenticity. My work is exactly like this, similar to the cutting of an emerald. With great care, respect, dedication, and skill, I carve and refine the stone, highlighting each woman's inner beauty in a unique and stunning way.

Each phase of this subtlety in cutting is like each step in the image consultancy. From discovering your personality, the unique characteristics of the stone, to the final polish, each step highlights a special quality and an unforgettable experience. At the end of this creative process, the emerald shines intensely, radiating vivid and bright colors. In the same way, you also shine with confidence, professionalism, and solidity, reflecting an even more authentic image that is truly yours, carefully crafted, and masterfully honed during your journey of self-discovery and personal growth.

A woman is a symbol of strength, just like the emerald. It is one of the most durable gems, symbolizing a woman's strength and resilience in the face of life's challenges. When we face difficulties, we transmit our inner strength, showing values and life experiences. The emerald also has characteristics of uniqueness and rarity, just like us women. Similar yet so different from each other, we become precious for being unique. When we think of the green color of the emerald, nature and growth immediately come to mind. We are always learning something new every day, constantly growing in all aspects of our lives.

Moreover, we seek to convey in our image the elegance and sophistication that the emerald represents. Therefore, our presence must go beyond the superficial impact; we must automatically express our elegance through our actions and confidence, revealing our true selves in the process.

How strong is your name?

Our name is the first and most enduring association people make with us. Our name is the central component of our identity and, by extension, our personal brand. It is a powerful tool for personalizing communication and creating a more intimate and direct connection. Everything we do, our actions, behaviors, and achievements, is associated with our name.

Just as an emerald is valued as a precious gem, our name expresses who we are throughout life. How do you believe people attribute characteristics to you?

Having a good name means we have a good reputation, which is very precious. When people remember our name, they associate it with a trustworthy, cheerful, friendly, charismatic, dedicated, intelligent person. They can also attribute negative traits, such as insecurity, unfriendliness, arrogance, and manipulation, among others.

Before someone introduces you to another person, they usually associate attributes as a reference. For example, "Let me introduce you to Bia, who is an excellent professional. She is very dedicated in what she does." Sometimes, you haven't even met a person yet, and you are already impressed by so many positive attributes, eager to have someone like that in your circle of friends.

Shirley Marie Williams, you may have never heard of this name. I have heard it quite a bit. But one thing we have in common, dear reader, is that we do not know this woman personally. So why am I mentioning her? For almost six years, many people have described her as: "Oh, she was an incredible woman, very friendly, strong-willed, smiling, and had a lot of faith." Indeed, you start to imagine what this woman would be like.

One day, I watched some videos of her with her family, and all these qualities were only reinforced: she seemed to be a very family-oriented and funny woman who would suddenly burst into laughter or call one of her children loudly and be in a good mood. Over time, I discovered some similarities between the two of us, like liking Michael Bublé and

Bruno Mars. They are small commonalities, but I never had the opportunity to meet her in person. Nevertheless, she gave me the greatest gift I could ever receive in my whole life: her son, my husband. As a bonus, I gained a brother-in-law and a father-in-law who are extensions of this incredible woman.

I am sure that people like the one I just described, by hearing about them, we already wish to be close and want to interact with them. It is this feeling I always have when I hear about her. The Bible says that having a good name is better than riches, and this is absolutely true. Riches fade away, but a good name will never be forgotten. Shirley made me love and admire her without ever having met her. The good name and reputation she built throughout her life are so strong that everyone who knew her, especially her children and husband, will never forget her.

Every August 16th since 2014 has become a difficult date for this new family of mine. But I immortalized my tribute to a woman who will never be forgotten here. After all, dressing yourself is not just about the external; to dress yourself, your qualities, values, and principles must be aligned with your image and make you unforgettable.

Conclusion

How long does a process take? What is the worth of facing so many challenges? The truth is we often want to skip the difficult phases. How often do we fail to realize that our insecurity, doubt, sadness, joy, and determination are all showing? In a world where building an image and maintaining authenticity is invaluable, being genuine is essential.

There was a time when image consulting was seen merely as help with dressing, but this book presents an innovative method: dressing yourself as a whole. No one can showcase their best or dress authentically without first discovering their uniqueness within.

Looking in the mirror and feeling confident about who we are is crucial. Understanding that there is a dress code for every occasion and having the confidence that our image conveys precisely what we want is fundamental. Developing an intentional image is important so that, when applying strategies, we don't lose our essence just to achieve results.

You can certainly move forward alone, but we can make everything much easier together. That's why, in my image consultancy, the results can be incredible, especially when accompanied by the expertise of my partner, Blenda. With her, you will understand how wonderful it is to know yourself and to perceive through someone else's eyes who we are, viewing us from the outside in. This strengthens the person we see in the mirror with more confidence and admiration, valuing our entire history and resilience.

Facing fear, even when feeling that nervous flutter, is essential. Internal changes reflect in our external appearance and can have a positive impact. Therefore, change! It is important to realize that understanding styles alone isn't enough for image success.

You must recognize that it's about the ensemble: hair, colors, lines and shapes, fabrics and textures, and what you intend to convey. Combining these elements results in a harmonious image.

Impressing others... Ah! So many people want to impress in the digital world, many forcing themselves to be who they are not, using branded clothes to create an impact. However, when meeting in person, the disappointment is inevitable. But imagine leaving a good impression just by being your authentic self. That's how I got to know my mother-in-law without ever seeing her in person. It felt as though we had been friends for ages simply because of the qualities unanimously attributed to her.

Be the best version of yourself, but don't forget to dress as your true self and be like an emerald, precious and unique.

In conclusion, our stories are continually strengthened by the support of other powerful women who provide the necessary backing to achieve our goals. These are women who believe in each other, comprehend our vulnerabilities, and are willing to fight and cry with and for us. I must register that without the unwavering support of my mother and sister, it would have been impossible to find the strength and courage to embrace this new beginning, the changes, and the good and bad moments up to now. The love and support I receive from them are fundamental and irreplaceable.

Women need other women! Together, we create a network of solidarity and strength where each achievement becomes a collective triumph. These women's presence in our lives strengthens us and inspires us to be the best versions of ourselves. This connection, mutual understanding, and support exchange allow us to grow and face challenges with determination.

Therefore, it's crucial to recognize and value the importance of these relationships. They are the foundation that sustains us, the shoulder that comforts us, and the hand that lifts us. The bond among women is a powerful link that transcends obstacles and leads us to realize our dreams.

This is not just a story of overcoming and starting anew that I'm sharing but also a tribute to the other women whose stories are narrated in this book. I am immensely grateful that they shared their challenges with us. Each story is a source of inspiration and an example of women's strength and resilience, illuminating the path for all of us.

Oh! But I must tell you how my story with Tyler turned out. Well, our story is still being written. On July 5, 2024, we celebrate five years of marriage, and this is just the beginning. We've adapted to our culture, language, and the many differences we have. What matters in this journey is how we write it daily with patience and love. Today, I love Tyler even more than I did on that first meeting in Brazil. He has helped me see myself with more courage and believe more in myself, and I am very grateful to have him by my side.

To you, dear reader, I leave my final message: never accept less than you deserve. We need and must be loved and respected, which is not a favor but a right we have. After all, our partners choose to love us, but it's up to us to decide how we allow ourselves to be treated. Do not accept anything less than a genuine love.

Dressing Yourself means being fully complete in your uniqueness.

Love yourself.
Respect yourself.
That's how you Dress Yourself!

About the Author

Viviane Williams is an entrepreneur from Brazil who is passionate about personal image and style. Her unique combination of skills and experiences makes her a versatile professional deeply passionate about the world of personal image and style. With an academic background in Administration, she has participated in a Branding Mentoring Program enhancing skills in personal branding.

Eager to delve deeper into Image and Style Consulting, Viviane pursued further education in Paris, one of the world's fashion capitals. There, she earned certification as an Image and Style Consultant, gaining valuable insights and a refined sense of fashion. She's ready to share her expertise with the world through her book.

Viviane Williams

As we reach the end of this book, I'd like to revisit your initial responses from the first pages and see how you would answer those same questions now after reading it.

How would you describe your image?

_____

_____

_____

_____

How important is your image to you?

_____

_____

_____

_____

_____

What results did you seek from reading this book?

_____

_____

_____

_____

_____

I want to get to know you and understand how I have helped. Please respond to this email: book@vivianewilliams.com.br

.